PENGU

THREE POI

Michael Hastings was brou
lives. At fifteen he commenc
tailoring, and in 1956 George Devine invited him to join the
Royal Court Theatre as an actor/writer. His plays are: *Don't
Destroy Me*, 1956; *Yes and After*, 1957; *The World's Baby*,
1964; *For the West (Congo)*, 1966; *Blue as His Eyes the Tin
Helmet He Wore*, 1966; *Lee Harvey Oswald: a far mean streak of
indepence brought on by negleck*, 1967; *The Silence of Saint-Just*,
1972; *The Cutting of the Cloth*, unperformed autobiographic
play, 1973; *For the West (Uganda)*, 1977; *Gloo Joo*, 1978;
Murder Rap, 1980; *Full Frontal*, 1980; *Midnite at the Starlite*,
1980; *Tom and Viv*, 1984; *Stars of the Roller State Disco*, 1984;
The Emperor (with Jonathan Miller), 1987.

Michael Hastings has won a number of awards in London
and New York, and is a Fellow of the Royal Geographical
Society. During visits to Brazil in 1974 and 1975, he wrote
two books, *And in the Forest the Indians* and *Bart's Mornings
and Other Tales of Modern Brazil*.

MICHAEL HASTINGS

THREE POLITICAL PLAYS

THE EMPEROR
with Jonathan Miller

FOR THE WEST (UGANDA)

LEE HARVEY OSWALD
a far mean streak of indepence
brought on by negleck

PENGUIN BOOKS

PENGUIN BOOKS

Published by the Penguin Group
27 Wrights Lane, London w8 5TZ, England
Viking Penguin Inc., 40 West 23rd Street, New York, New York 10010, USA
Penguin Books Australia Ltd, Ringwood, Victoria, Australia
Penguin Books Canada Ltd, 2801 John Street, Markham, Ontario, Canada L3R 1B4
Penguin Books (NZ) Ltd, 182–190 Wairau Road, Auckland 10, New Zealand

Penguin Books Ltd, Registered Offices: Harmondsworth, Middlesex, England

The Emperor by Ryszard Kapuściński originally published in the United Kingdom by
Quartet Books. Translated by William R. Brand and Katarzyna Mroczkowska-Brand.
Adapted for the stage by Michael Hastings and Jonathan Miller
Copyright © Ryszard Kapuściński, 1978. English translation copyright © Ryszard
Kapuściński, 1983. Adaptation copyright © Michael Hastings and Jonathan Miller, 1987
Produced by permission of Harcourt Brace Jovanovich, Inc. First published in the English
language by Harcourt Brace Jovanovich, Inc.

For the West (Uganda) first published by Penguin Books 1980
Copyright © Michael Hastings, 1980

Lee Harvey Oswald first published by Penguin Books 1966
Copyright © Michael Hastings, 1966

This collection published in Penguin Books 1990
1 3 5 7 9 10 8 6 4 2
Introduction copyright © Michael Hastings, 1990
All rights reserved

All performing rights in these plays are fully protected, and permission to perform must be
obtained in advance from Jonathan Clowes Ltd, 22 Prince Albert Road, London NW1 7ST

Made and printed in Great Britain by
Cox and Wyman Ltd, Reading, Berks.
Filmset in Linotron Bembo by
Rowland Phototypesetting Ltd, Bury St Edmunds, Suffolk

CONTENTS

INTRODUCTION

The problem with the bromide 'all plays are political' is that it became enshrined in a cheerful universality. It is the kind of homily a nation can fall asleep beside, only to wake up and learn that this jewel of self-evidence has been stolen clean away in a swagbag stuffed with other so-called rights. I believe there may soon come a time when theatre will need more than vigilance to keep even the most incontestable slogan.

Of course, few can doubt that all plays are political in so far as they dare to dramatize ideas and parade the collision of human events. Even the immeritorious bilge of the latest musical that aims to claw profit from an unwitting public cannot conceal its own politics of social contempt.

The problem now is rather different. In a liberal/capitalist environment too many plays in the past have kidnapped the term 'political' to justify their agitprop. Meanwhile, other works that claim a degree of artistic merit have failed to scale the high ground of political debate. Both kinds of writing seem totally valid, but a divide has been created. We are now back in the crucible of Chekhov's argument that plays must either solve a problem (i.e., lean to agitprop) or they must lay out evenly all the complications of a problem. Enemies of modern theatre will make great play with this divide. It is possible to foresee a time when both kinds will suffer the same common enemy. When one looks back it isn't too difficult to find the origins of this divide. There have been enough plays hellbent on imposing political debate on their audience – for instance, Middleton's *A Game at Chess*, or Fielding's *Don Quixote in England*, or Toller's expressionistic *Masses and Man*. Not unexpectedly, these plays became notorious more for the speed with which they were closed down by the authorities than for their intrinsic merit. On the other hand, there are plays that suffer the misfortune of having politics imposed upon them, even though their merit is impossible to deny. Examples are Ibsen's *Ghosts*, O'Casey's *The Plough and the Stars*, and Havel's *The Memorandum*. These playwrights did not set out to write pieces that would close theatres. But all of these plays have at some point in history felt the full force of state violence and suppression. For a moment we can glimpse the power of mocking political theatre because Walpole could not put up with Fielding's sharp tongue. Václav Havel still lives in Prague, but all productions of his satire have been banned for the last twenty years. And yet the creative intention behind such plays is quite different, and the playwrights could not be further apart in their individual politics. This suggests to me that it is not only wrong to allow agitprop the exclusive use of the term 'political', it is positively an act of disservice to other kinds of play. We run the risk of letting our enemies divide our culture on the stage, when we should be only too aware of the deeply enshrined politics found in the tawdriest musical show. Whilst we hum and haw over Pirandello's rightist politics, any number of drivelling farces gaily get by which exhibit even more loathsome emotional fascism.

Are we losing sight of some certain but baser element of communication here? For example, it has been argued instructively that among newspapers in Britain the most overtly political is the *Sun*. This deeply committed if lurid tabloid of our daily lives has ten million readers, and it arrives on one's doorstep in the cunning disguise of a gobbing nutter's comic. Conceivably, a serious playwright who seeks an audience may have to engineer a pattern of responses less associated with high moral ground and more akin to a mode of commonality. This does not, of course, exclude merit; more importantly, it means understanding that agitprop may have become a form of mandarin writing, ultimately elitist and sectarian.

These three plays published here, which cover a period of twenty years or so, are among those which from time to time find politics imposed upon them. There was always in the writing a desire for intrinsic merit, no matter how small. If anything, at the time of writing my chief concern was to target as wide an audience as possible. And I believed my tools were the normal creative weapons of a playwright committed to his time. But when I look at the fragile voyages these plays have made, I understand that they were written not solely to entertain, nor to elicit cries from the converted in the mandarin house. And yet when they have failed, in some instances, to find the intended breadth of audience, no self-righteous indignation on the playwright's behalf can possibly exonerate him.

Although *The Emperor* can be staged in Poland, Israel and Iran, there is as much chance of seeing it in Addis Ababa as there is hope that Coptic camels may ice-skate. *For the West (Uganda)* can indeed have a Students' Union production in Nairobi, but the director of the Kampala National Theatre risks his life if he stages it there. *Lee Harvey Oswald* can be performed in Mexico City for three months, but it cannot be presented on any US stage even after twenty years. For a dizzy moment this might lead one to the dubious notion that any play is 'political' if it is denied a production in the homeland of the play's setting. Is there some kind of ultramontane conspiracy that keeps these plays out of their landscapes of origin? Let us keep a sense of humility here. Surely nobody is suggesting these plays might create social upheaval?

If plays were such a potent force, then modern revolutionary armies would be storming across borders armed only with tankfuls of actors and props, brandishing scripts by various sultry playwrights whose self-righteousness had never been more refreshingly vindicated. Mad-dog regimes and loony fascist generals would topple overnight, and the liberators could roll back evil for a nonce of stagey poncers. Alas, sense prevails, and the problem with a play is that even if it can bring down a government this will by no means guarantee a full house every night. A more pragmatic way of identifying political plays is to concede that certain plays can be thought dangerous at varying times, even though their writers may never have envisaged such a response.

However, one should spare a thought for the playwright and his potentially dangerous play. Is he to be shot? Exiled? Even put on a manufacturers' blacklist and forbidden ever again to touch the keys of a word processor? I'm not even so sure playwrights are that brave in this country. When Charles Lamb attended his own first night in London, the abuse and vilification at the end of the show was so violent that Lamb joined in and screamed the loudest imprecations at himself just in case he was recognized as the author. Of course, there *have been* playwrights in modern history who have suffered persecution. Paul Kornfeld, Walter Hasenclever, Ernst Toller, perhaps even Ödön von Horváth, died, in one way or another, as victims of the Nazi regime (although the Third Reich can't be held entirely to blame for the fork lightning that felled Horváth in Paris).

Certain points can be pinned down. A play can prove volatile at the right nervous moment. Unaligned playwrights can be seen to be dangerous when their work is unexpectedly abducted by a faction's ulterior political motives. But theatre is not a pure form. It is communally based. And since it is a predominantly shared art experience, all do not uniformly seek high moral ground on the stage. After all, a theatre without an audience is a pile of bricks. And playwrights who have thought themselves superior to their punters have died lonely lives of bitter contemplation on a world filled with people they hold in contempt. And because there exists a condition of practical vulgarity in stage work, it might be of some use to describe a more lowly but generous arena. 'If theatre wants to find itself needed,' wrote Artaud, 'it must present everything in love, crime, war and madness.' If only it could be elevated to such jaw-struck fine trinkum.

On one side, there is the case that agitprop should remain the mother of all political stages. This may run the risk of producing a theatre of self-immolation – works of no lasting value – but that is the nature of the struggle. It is a form of artistic sacrifice against the crimes of the time. There is also the theatre of excellence and imagination. Neither type of play is exclusive to the needs of the proletariat, or has an inalienable right to high moral ground. In between these poles it may be possible to uncover a common area that is vulgar but cognate.

Nobody can sensibly believe ancient Greek theatre got across to the goat-drovers and priests alike unless they already possessed some low knowledge of the plays. Here were three or four actors behind stone masks, standing erect in *cothurni* boots, singing rather than speaking perhaps, and yet they made this vulgar knowledge a moment of ceremonial intensity. Characters in these ancient plays rarely had fictitious names, they were known tabloid creations. These stories of great trials between gods and kings remained cognate because the goat-drover knew these names. Thus in the stone auditorium the audience had a glimpse of popular mythology made flesh. And if, as Malraux asserts, 'myth is the celebration of the people', we may have stumbled across a seed-bed for the vulgar but cognate.

Thus, instead of assuming high moral ground, it might even be possible to change our view of political theatre. It may seem ludicrous to use the phrase 'low moral ground', but here perhaps is a common area where horror retains the majestic, and cruelty becomes ceremonial. The goat-drover and the priest apprehend with low knowledge. These are common stereotypes on the stage; the audience has enough tabloid nous about these gods and kings not to be deceived. In a sense, Ajax or Hecuba or Creon has already been found out before the play begins. Their biographies are hearsay, and although biography itself on the stage may only be a fiction on crutches, the early Greek playwrights had no shame about this.

Inevitably, it is impossible for humankind not to see the low and absurd in the theatrical parade. And somewhere between Aristotle's idea that the theatre should show us how our world ought to be and Jarry's notion that art is a stuffed crocodile, there exists perhaps this area of vulgar apprehension. Political theatre may not be a venue where actors do their utmost to disabuse their audiences of their convictions. It may be a place where the lowest moral claims are indulged with a flight of imagination. To borrow from Karl Kraus, the real political truths are those that can be invented.

Not long ago, on an African trip, I climbed to the ridge above Lake Malawi. Below was a steep fall. Below, the water shaved itself with a dazzling stillness; only from time to time did a sailing cloud reflect itself on the lapis calm. My companion was an African playwright who has since died. He talked about another writer. The authorities had denied this writer everything. He was being systematically turned into a non-person. He couldn't write his articles for papers. His teaching post had been taken from him. He was denied access to any publishers. So he wrote one last short story in Malawi. In the story he climbs up to this same ridge above the lake. He is determined to kill himself. When he gets to the top, he discovers a long queue of people lined up to the very edge. Just as the writer is about to jump, the last person in the queue taps him on his shoulder. He tells the writer, 'You can't commit suicide here. You've got to take your turn like the rest of us. You've got to stand in line and wait behind me.'

My companion was not certain I'd grasped the meaning of this short story. It wasn't another tale of fashionable despair. It was more than that. He told me: 'This was a story of political hope. It was a cry of hope. Because less than that would be humanly intolerable.'

In other words, the writer's true inspiration was the expectation of nothing. For it is such an implacable indignity to be told you cannot even give away your own life without the decorum of community obligations.

'What playwrights in the West,' asked my companion, 'have been reduced to that?'

A question which makes for cold follicles on the back of the head. You glance around at your contemporaries and our (rightly) subsidized theatre, and it is possible to glimpse that we are writing in a late warm climate that has briefly and wickedly flowered like a nuclear summer. Meanwhile, no one observes the movement of a coming ice-age. Few enough voices rise up to remind us that the next tyranny will be gradual. No sudden shock to the nation's system with mass eugenics. They have carefully learnt, now. It will be done gently, with courteous restraint. And years may have to pass by. As for the plays that warned, they may well look like soiled semaphors from a once safe anchorage in the past. New people will shrug and ask, what did they achieve, those plays of anger? Those medicine-plays that treated the audience like patients in a social surgery? Why did no one listen? Is it because lemmings are not known for visiting the theatre on the night they scramble over the cliff edge?

But we know that silence kills history. If no one speaks out, do we find philosophy in tea-leaves? The artist in the teeth of his times may die happy with his aesthetic code of practice, but if an ice-age lies ahead not even the most gifted but politically mute genius should act as if it were inevitable.

These three plays need the shape of people in legend. They reach to realize these people in the low moral ground of an invented world. They are about the death of power. In one case, death by slow decay once the oligarchy has gone blind. In another, a nation's suicide under a regime born out of a former colonial rule. Lastly, the assassin observed as a nation's dupe. All three plays are set outside, in a wider world, where the playwright is, as it were, writing away from home. I hope these plays have slipped the shackles of parochial British mannerism. Playwrights know to their cost the indifference of managements to scripts that try to face the outside world. Such are the constraints, it is difficult enough to get one stage play mounted every five years. Novels trespass over continents and ride sea-horses of the mind; incautious though it may be for playwrights to attempt the same, if they did not, then the stage would have to own up to a relinquished domain.

The Emperor

Few books inspire a playwright to rush out into the street and chant from it out loud. *The Emperor* by Ryszard Kapuściński was first published in 1983 in England. It had already been recognized in Europe as a remarkable piece of creative journalism, but the initial lit-crit British response was narrow and reserved. Some distinguished writers including Ian McEwan, Caryl Philips and Salman Rushdie rose to its defence, but a view persisted that here was just another book about the fall of Emperor Haile Selassie. But Kapuściński is something more than just a reporter. Certainly he's been a regular figure in the flock of international foreign correspondents who descend on every new hot spot of 'world crisis'. He's been employed by the Polish Press Agency as their star contributor, and there have been sightings of him in Angola and Mexico, in Uganda and Iran, in Ethiopia and the Philippines. In one sense Kapuściński has travelled almost everywhere on our behalf, filing his stories and cabling bulletins from impossible war-torn bivouacs.

In due course, Kapuściński published a portrait of Teheran in a state of revolution, *Shah of Shahs* (1985), and a study of the war in Angola, *Another Day of Life* (1987), and he has promised a further book about Amin in the final days of the Kakwa regime in Uganda. Gradually it dawned on us that we had here a distinctive artist who created through and in spite of the disciplines of straight reportage. It was as if a modern-day Suetonius was born equipped with Robert Capa's camera eye for the fundamental details of a nation when it appears to commit suicide. And yet, on closer inspection, none of these can be called absolute facts. A strong imaginative element has crept into this work. The pages appear like frozen shots of verbal horror such as only Robert Capa could have created with his Nikon lens. There were phrases and moments no strict historian could find, and these were turned into a form of art by the urgency of the lived experience of Kapuściński. And in the days of the Emperor Domitian, any librarian could have handed you the c.v. of the Imperial Titus, but it took Suetonius to give us Titus at the end of a long day when he had done nothing of any good for any person. For Suetonius records for us: 'Titus stood alone by the palace window and murmured, "I have lost a day."' This snapshot of an autocrat belongs to Suetonius and not to the historian. It was this quality in Kapuściński that drew me first to the book about the diminutive King of Kings and descendant of Solomon, Haile Selassie.

In 1985 I asked the Royal Court Theatre if I could set up a workshop with a group of actors to try to stage Kapuściński's *The Emperor*. On the surface the book is a series of taped interviews with the last servants and courtiers who attended the old palace in Addis Ababa during the collapse of the reign.

Although the Emperor had been stripped of much of his retinue, the sprinklers on the April-green lawns still bicycled through the air, and the chained leopards were regularly fed. The corridors of the grand old building now echoed. Mysteriously, all the palace gates were locked from the outside. Only one old bedservant stayed with the Emperor. What was in truth a military coup by a section of the Emperor's own tribe also contained strong seeds of a revisionist form of Stalinist government. But the leaders of the revolt remained in such awe of the Emperor that they refused to give their names or ranks, and some only became known to the general public months later. But they had made up their minds to isolate the Emperor in such a way that nothing on the surface appeared untoward. Even in these reduced circumstances, with ever-decreasing numbers of courtiers, every bureaucratic detail still functioned in the old palace. The Emperor still gave his approval to matters. He could not leave the building, but he could still wear his ornate uniforms. He could feed the leopards, but his telephone, that once called Geneva or Washington, would not ring any further out than to the chief clerk in the post office. If he wished to stand on the royal balcony he was free to do so. Indeed, he could formally salute the distant traffic passing in the road outside. And sometimes the people even waved back at his fragile gestures. Especially the handful of tourists at the entrance to the Hilton Hotel.

The voices of the courtiers in *The Emperor* have a certain blind martyrdom about them. Kapuściński wrote to me: 'They are trembling voices, trying to convince us they are unable to understand why all this tragedy had to happen to them.'

It took some months for the theatre to confirm the stage rights. Meantime, as yet unknown to the Royal Court, Jonathan Miller had also expressed plans to produce this book on the stage. And so Max Stafford-Clark, Artistic Director of the Royal Court, asked Jonathan and myself to take a workshop together. It was a fortunate break which could be fitted into Jonathan's schedule, and an opportunity to tempt this brilliant director back to the Court.

During the initial casting days I felt we needed a company which in some way reflected the strange demands of the narrative of the book. There was, for example, an elderly courtier who spent all his life on his knees wiping the urine that untrained royal dogs left on dignitaries' shoes. There was another strange creature who spent his life amidst fifty-two royal cushions, kept solely for the purpose of making sure the feet of the Emperor, who was of small stature, were never left dangling in the air – particularly when the Emperor took his high thrones around the countryside.

By chance, I had seen a remarkable Syrian-born actor, Nabil Shaban, in previous months. He worked frequently with the foremost theatre group for the disabled, Graeae Company. Although he remains almost completely confined to a wheelchair, he has a distinctive acting style of grace and soul. And it was Nabil who first came to my mind for the workshop period.

As soon as we started to pare down the book into a script, it became obvious that here was no 'Denver boot' of naturalism. There is hardly one exchange of dialogue, and barely a moment of interaction between characters. We all found we were dealing with a kind of purely narrated stage-work, a language of telling, rather like that of the ancient African memorizers of tribal knowledge. It is a tradition of stage-work which possibly goes back to the Sophoclean drama, and to Aesop. The weight of these individual stories that make up the book had to acquire a certain stillness of delivery and an evocation of memory. Jonathan had initial ideas of placing the performers before great sheets of white paper, as in Irving Penn's famous series of photographic portraits. But the actual text also hinted of other matters. Yes, the subject was Ethiopia, but casual hints also indicated a wickedly indirect description of other regimes of modern times – in particular the late Polish government under Edward Gierek. Often inside *The Emperor* there is uncovered an impish East European tone of Broch and Kraus. And thus the designer Richard Hudson joined our curious little world of Polish politics and African tribal memorizers, and he presented us with a design for a set filled with half-doors, tiny box windows and crooked cupboards that rose six inches from the floor. All painted in a shading grey. Jonathan determined now that our company should wear plain suits and ties and acquire the look of bureaucratic souls in a pantomime of mnemonic grief. A hint of 'social surrealism' was being naturally created.

But surrealism is an old dog now. After Breton and Duchamp, it now performs tricks for promo videos. Surrealism has become a kind of sport (wasn't it 'Marvellous' Marvin Hagler who said, 'When they open up my skull they'll find inside a boxing glove'?). Was this all we had achieved in the rehearsal period? A matrix of style placed over these voices snared in tragedy? Indeed, was this even *tragedy*?

According to Suetonius, the Emperor Titus lost a day of usefulness. But in the old palace in Addis Ababa, our courtiers discover they have lost more than that, a whole life has passed by. And yet Kapuściński has chosen to give them very little self-reflection. These figures possess an ordinariness which does not presume to measure up to tragedy. Their grief and pity do not belong to tragic heights. They are witnesses to a disaster, but, rather like antic termites, they possess strength only in unity. There is a choral nature about them. Thus, instead of talking about tragedy and the fall of great figures, Kapuściński is concerned with memory. And I realized that our characters have been deliberately denied the ancient accoutrements of classical tragedy. They possess a forgetfulness which can only lead them to exile, whereas remembrance is the secret of redemption.

But in a modern world only the crass will look for atonement or redemption when confronted with Auschwitz or Hiroshima. The idea of classical tragedy can make one feel a fool. It may be possible to fathom the mimed scream of, say, Oedipus with a degree of abstraction. But hubris and catharsis, and stone masks in ancient sunlit amphitheatres? Surely it is the idea of *fall* that has now replaced the Eumenides? I don't quite mean the story of the sky-jumper whose parachute won't open as he tumbles to his death, and how he fights in those final seconds to control the harness and save his life. That is an accidental death. I mean that in our time one is encouraged to reduce the idea of ancient Greek tragedy to some kind of psychological rationale. It has been argued that all tragedy on the ancient forums can be reduced to exogamy or endogamy, with a flash of regicide in between. Therefore, either we have lost the rules that enable us to grasp tragic perception, or this type of perception has itself become an irrelevance.

When I embarked on *The Emperor* by Kapuściński, I began to understand tragedy better through these banal courtiers in the old palace, whose only longings are for the dream of an unimpeachable past. For no matter the enormity of their crimes, it becomes almost impossible to invoke great hubris here. And I grew to suspect that for Kapuściński these courtly creatures, swallows without a winter, can only be observed with an implacable dismay.

Dismay instead of tragedy? How have we contrived to bring down our most profound elaborations of the past to what seems like trivia? The answer to some of this may lie in Saint-Just's notorious speech to the Assembly in 1793. 'No one can rule innocently,' he declared. 'To be a King is a crime in itself,' he insisted. The measure of over-kill Saint-Just employed can still exact a wry smile. But the importance of his meaning cannot be shaken. For in a single speech he made it virtually impossible to invoke grief or pity or any of the other accoutrements of classical drama. Saint-Just continued: 'The human heart advances from Nature to violence, from violence to morality.' Thereupon, tragedy itself had to be re-investigated. In a modern light, there are grosser images than any parachutist in the process of fall or any King Louis. In a modern light, what kind of response can one make when confronted with the death ovens of Auschwitz? What do you say when you observe the stained shadow of a man on a wall in Hiroshima which is all that is left of the evaporated body in the atomic heat? When Saint-Just trumpeted, 'No one can rule innocently,' I believe he was asking us to reconsider all our tragic fables. In real terms only a madman would raise himself to grief and pity over Louis. In real terms only the most foolish shepherd or street beggar is going to weep for Clytemnestra. In real terms only an audience of fools would want to honour the reign of Kapuściński's *The Emperor*. And if Saint-Just is anything to go by, after morality has failed there comes an anger. And after anger, a realization that the idea of human happiness is a social force. Perhaps, confronted with the enormities of modern crime this century, all of us are beginning to die with greater humility. According to Malraux, from 'the Emperor made God' we have turned to 'God made man'. It suggests a journey of multiplying awareness in the direction of 'man made human'.

Throughout the opening weeks of the production there were nightly demonstrations by different groups outside the theatre. Occasionally there were busloads of Rastafarians from Manchester who believed we were desecrating the God-like attributes of this Amharic descendant of Solomon, Haile Selassie. There were also impeccably dressed pro-royalist Ethiopians who arrived with the most elegant banners held aloft, and who departed with sulky grace into large limousines waiting nearby. There is no doubt the Rastafarian movement is a genuine form of spiritual regeneration. It was started by Leonard Howell and Archibald Dunkley in the Caribbean in response to a natural demand to find an African Homeland based on love and brotherhood. It professes a quasi-racial interpretation of history, claiming not only that the Pharaohs were black, but also Solomon and Jesus Christ. One day to come, the government of the African Zion might well be a theocracy. Be that as it may, it requires a certain leap of imagination to believe that the Emperor Haile Selassie was directly descended from the Queen of Sheba. There is no evidence anywhere to suggest that the empire of Axum (*c.* 500 BC) was in any way a progenitor of the empire formed by Menelik (*c.* AD 1890) in Addis Ababa. But it remained an uneasy and unnatural world of theatre when the old palace on the stage itself was the target of the exilic cries and shouts that filtered into the auditorium.

Working with Jonathan Miller on this particular play was an added bonus. Miller has a method of dissecting the commonplace and discovering with delight a form of bizarre humour. He often leaps upon the prosaic to turn it into a moment of reckless laughter, as if mirth itself was the best revenge against the minatory void. He is inspired, tireless, sometimes silly, it is like watching a poet on a trampoline.

At times during the rehearsals it was difficult to tell whether Kapuściński's fine sadnesses were running aground on cheaper shores of comedy. But there is always serious laughter. Albeit a form of revenge, it didn't destroy the weight of the words. I make no mistake when I say that Kapuściński has clearly denied us tragedy in his book. I detect a certain coldness in his resolve. Yet, in a personal sense, it has made me more aware of the tragic mould. Although classical tragedy had a place in a world filled with God-like certainties, it still remains inconceivable that we have lost sight of this. If we lived in a world where tragedy did not exist, laughter would become the sound of horror. If the concept of tragedy was taken from us, laughter would acquire the burden and the ambiguity of the most unbearable pain, as in the cult of the Maya, where the skinned features of a young child are poured over the grinning face of the jaguar. Laughter alone would then revenge nothing; all we would hear would be the braying of blind mouths.

At the close of the rehearsal period the whole company felt we had achieved, if not a tragic tone, at least an implacable sadness. By the end of the play all that is left on the stage is these memory-engorged voices. And what have these voices brought to us? Have these gliding figures of elegant tales forgotten nothing but the one vital element that can lead them to safety in the streets outside? Allow that each witness can recount without guile or self-reflection the chronicle of his days, why is it he can offer up not one word to mitigate atonement? Kapuściński is discreet here. He disallows them catharsis. And, I suspect, as an artist he steps back, leaving us with these choral invocations, a litany of poltroons if you like; and if Kapuściński rages, it is with a cold anger.

For the West (Uganda)

Of course there are national borders in East Africa, but the principal divisions of grazing land are still tribal. The war between Idi Amin and the southern part of Uganda was fought on tribal grounds as the President-for-Life retreated.

I stopped for a brief time on the Jinja road into Uganda. It served as a main route of exodus to Kenya at the Tororo junction. A few lorries piled with broken furniture and decimated families still headed east into Kenya. There was a general mood of despair. This particular part of Uganda has an unusual history. In 1902 the British colonial overlord had earmarked the land, some four hundred square miles, for a future settlement of European Zionists. Had that happened, those lorries of decimated families would have been met with yet another border, with perhaps kibbutzim walls and gun emplacements. Out on these stubborn green plains the narrow-haunched Zebu cattle graze alongside newly imported fatstock, and herds gather for shade at midday. Clearly, all state borders in East Africa are arbitrary lines, political dreams of geographers, ripe only for picking and plunder by tribal irredentists.

I had wanted for some time to write a play about our interpretation of Idi Amin. I wasn't concerned so much with the personality of a tyrant as with the idea of a ruler who had been educated mainly by the British army, in the King's African Rifles. For between 1971 and 1978, Idi Amin lurched from a friendly fool we could buy off with untold sales of arms to a monster of depravity who murdered 300,000 southern Ugandans and kept morsels of enemy bodies in his fridge for midnight snacks. British journalists made a meal of this. The cartoonists were rampant.

It was a fascinating experience to watch the response to Amin. We had set him up as an obedient and greedy client in the arms trade, but as soon as the Ugandan purse split and Amin's international borrowing power was turned off, our response was a field-day of calculated racism vilely directed not only at the man but at an entire East African community now brought to its knees. Britain's public response to the latter part of the Amin rule bordered on a form of mass dementia. We had failed to identify a Pol Pot among the Republican movement in Belfast, we hadn't even located an Irgun Genghis Khan in British-occupied Palestine, but sure as eggs is eggs we'd at last found a 'black Hitler' in Africa. Other friends in various parts of Africa pointed out to me how virulent was this pastime. The racialism slavered from our lips. We could barely contain ourselves. African friends of mine asked: was this how Belgium salivated over the fall of Lumumba? Or how France wallowed in the death of Boumedienne? No, of course it wasn't. I had a vision of our own very British sickness. Those rabid cartoons and leaders were coals to our bigot hearths.

After Independence in 1962, Amin's career accelerated through the King's African Rifles. Within two years he had become Deputy Commander of the Ugandan Army under President Milton Obote. Although there was a Parliamentary Legislature of 80 seats, Obote distanced himself from the southern tribal kingdoms, and under a scheme called the Common Man's Charter, central government confiscated a 60-per-cent interest in all major financial and industrial concerns in the country. Soon the British government showed renewed disdain for the Obote regime. Obote was involved in certain gold and ivory smuggling operations from out of Zaire. But World Bank and allied American and Japanese interests quickly realized that this was a perfect undeveloped young nation ripe for capital expansion. Its principal cash crop, coffee, amounted to 75 per cent of the Ugandan agriculture. Copper, the prime mining product, was already in the hands of the Japanese. All the country needed was a stiff return to military rule and rejection of any Common Man's Charter nonsense, and the country could become a debtor client in the world of international borrowing. After all, income per capita stood at £150, but the national product was capable of turning over £2 billion. Clearly, there were pickings galore.

In 1971, when Obote was out of the country, Amin led a small army of Anyanya Sudanese. He captured Kampala and Jinja. A number of British and Israeli military advisers, intent on toppling the socialist world of Obote, accompanied Amin. An interim government was announced. These were heady times for Amin. Britain and Israel, with the support of the World Bank, provided shipments of arms and military equipment. Amin set about an immediate and systematic slaughter of Lango and Acholi tribes that had been loyal to Obote. Amin made sudden visits to Europe, and one particularly infelicitous descent on the Vatican. All these plane flights fuelled in Tel Aviv. Within three months Britain had recognized Amin's junta. Events moved so swiftly, it wasn't possible for the West to grasp or even care about the nature of the beast it had invented.

All legal rights were suspended and members of the armed forces were empowered to arrest or shoot on sight any suspected opponent of the junta. The powers of the judiciary and police were usurped by the secret police, the State Research Bureau, who were above the law. The Chief Justice of Uganda, Benedicto Kiwanuka, was bludgeoned to death. The annual OAU conference, scheduled to meet in Kampala, hastily shifted to Addis.

In the space of four years Amin had a number of dreams that did untold damage to the country. One dream ordered him to expel all 32,000 Asians within ninety days. Most of them held UK passports already, and although the expulsion was applauded by many African states, it was a pre-emptive strike of racism from a junta toppling into fascism. Amin reorganized the administrative divisions of Uganda into ten provinces and thirty-eight districts. Each province came under a military governor directly answerable to Amin. Meanwhile irrational events collided inside the country. Russia sent teams of surgeons but there were no hospitals. Libya supplied dozens of pilots but there were hardly any planes fit to fly. Admiral-in-Chief Amin decreed the formation of a Ugandan navy, and the American Congress for Racial Equality (CORE) made him a life member.

Shortly after the Archbishop of Uganda was murdered, Amin found financial backing from the Arab emirates. We were witnessing the Western implantation of a form of military fascism on unknown territory. Worse, this had been done under an umbrella of loans and military hardware. Worse still, nobody seemed to understand the implications of pitting old royalist tribes (the Baganda) against Sudanic-speaking northern tribes who were a disenfranchised people of Muslim faith. Amin's presence had introduced the most extraordinary variety of inter-tribal factions; on top of this, the man was a strutting carbon-copy of a British army officer who had risen through the ranks. Underneath the anger of neighbouring states in Africa, Amin was still safe with new Arab funds. Presented with a booming world coffee market, he was unlikely to alienate all the tribes of the southern agricultural belt. At the bottom line, Amin could escape north with his Kakwa units, his Muslim foot soldiers, for they had always been the outcasts of Uganda. Everything stemmed from this single erratic figure. This was fascism obscenely erected across a fragile land, with a very thin veneer of British judiciary and comic inventiveness, but outright opprobrium was not in any way guaranteed. The world had already got used to our little British schemes about 'ruling the unruleable'. Attention became more focused on our behaviour in East Africa as Amin toppled from power. In our folly we imagined we had supplanted an embryonic socialism with a friendly grinning giant festooned with a cod lot of British medals. In reality, we had stumbled upon a feudal grenade which went off in our faces. We thought we had a puppet buffoon, instead he turned out to be a tribal fascist who represented aggrieved moieties from the north. In this part of East Africa we had exchanged one form of law for another kind we knew even less about, *ignotum per ignotius*.

I wrote *For the West (Uganda)* as a form of redress. It is a play which may never see the light in Kampala, but if it has achieved anything, it has at least offered up a portrait of a colonial mother country determined by any means to keep a grip on the East African shelf, even if this meant imposing fascism on a nation already divided by tribal borders.

We have laughed hugely at Idi Amin, and now he is demoted to the nether world of a political pariah; but still faintly can we discern – not without a residue of guilt – the echo of his killing laughter from a mouthful of blood, and it is tossed back at us like a malign child of our own making.

Lee Harvey Oswald

President John Kennedy was assassinated in Dallas on Friday 22 November 1963. The open car had just turned west into Dealey Plaza and passed the Book Depository building. Less than forty-five minutes later a man was involved in the shooting of a patrol cop about three miles from the scene. The police officer, J. D. Tippit, fell dead beside his car, and a man ran into a nearby cinema. When police entered the cinema, the man produced a handgun but was overpowered. The man was Lee Oswald, an employee at the Book Depository. But this all happened some three miles away from Dealey Plaza. And yet within a few hours the Dallas police had found a cheap rifle and some used shells on an upper floor of the Book Depository, and the entire Dallas police force seemed determined to pin blame for both murders on the hapless Oswald in their custody. Lee Oswald was held in police custody for forty-eight hours. On the Sunday morning he was being taken through the basement of the Dallas Police and Courts Building in handcuffs when a nightclub owner, Jack Ruby, lunged out of a crowd of police officers and journalists and shot Oswald dead with a single bullet.

As most of this was being shown live on television across the whole of America it was not surprising that sections of the public wanted some kind of explanation for these violent acts which so rudely interrupted a seamless diet of soaps and Kreem Wheaty breakfast commercials. Was all this real? Who were the Dallas police? Which communist was responsible for this? As for the slain President, from a head-count it seems that less than 20 per cent of the American people had bothered to vote for him, yet it was no easy task to find a motive for killing him. The US government responded by setting up a commission of inquiry which involved over 250 witnesses and two million words of testimony and published its findings a year later.

The twenty-six volumes of *Hearings before the President's Commission on the Assassination of President Kennedy*, otherwise known as the Warren Report, became a best-seller. People pored over the most minute details in search of these sad and blighted characters such as Oswald and Ruby. But the main purpose of the Warren Report was to steady the American nerve. The Report was only interested in Oswald's guilt. It was desperate to exonerate the Dallas police force. And it was determined to place all the national blame on the theory of the lone assassin. Nothing else was considered good enough for the American people. On the surface it looked like an exhaustive inquiry. Yes, maybe one man *could have* fired all three, four, five or was it six bullets? Certainly, one crucial bullet *could have* passed through both the President and the Texan Governor in front of him, and to be sure this bullet *could have* bounced against bone and tissue in two humans, and then fallen out of them both in a near pristine state. And there were details like the measurements of Oswald's cadaver. Apparently he was five feet nine inches tall when arrested. But a couple of days later when he was put into his coffin he was five feet six inches.

The Report took two million words to compile, but nobody deemed it of any value to add an index to this investigative industry. It took several months before certain small voices began to raise doubts. As time has gone by, over forty studies of the Report have been published, and one state-sponsored investigation of the claims in the Report has taken new evidence. And gradually it becomes apparent that although this work may not be wholly fiction, it is at the least a monumental essay in public appeasement. But, having said that, it remains impossible to disengage Messrs Kennedy, Oswald, Ruby and Tippit from the immortal headlock of the most unlikely association in modern times.

I first went to Dallas after reading the twenty-six volumes of the Warren Report. One of the most compelling problems about Lee Oswald is just how he could have made a leisurely exit from the Book Depository, walked seven blocks, changed his mind and taken a bus back to where he started from, taken a taxi to his rooming house and stopped there a few minutes, and then walked about a mile to the spot where he confronted the police officer, all in the space of forty-three minutes. After a couple of days in Dallas I realized I wasn't the only outsider trying to follow this tortuous route by car. I met up with four souls in the space of a week who were equally determined to look for Lee Harvey Oswald and follow his unlikely footsteps. Eventually a patrol officer stopped my car and asked for some ID.

'Where you from, sir?'

'England.'

'Which state that?'

'England, Europe,' I murmured.

'Aw – Great Britain. Why didn't ya say, sir?' He smiled at me. 'Great Britain in Europe! Sure.'

I explained to the officer that I was following Lee Oswald's supposed route on that fateful day. He seemed to understand immediately. There were no more questions. As far as he was concerned, it made absolute sense to stumble across this chap who had travelled six thousand miles to ring the doorbell of Oswald's last known rooming house.

'Everybody wants to come to Dallas to talk about Lee Oswald,' said the officer and got back in his patrol car, fully satisfied with my explanation. Inside my car I closed the window and boosted the air-cool. What on earth was I doing there? What extraordinary compulsion had made me go this far? If I'd told that officer about the discrepancy in Lee Oswald's true height between life and death, would he have been just as understanding?

Some months after, I went to a supper at the American

Embassy in London. Outside the house I got to talking with the American agents on duty. It turned out one of them had ridden on a car behind Kennedy on the day of the assassination. The agent had also read extracts from the Warren Report. He said, 'It don't matter how hard you look at it. How many times you run it through your head. It never happened the way they say it did.'

The most common argument in favour of the fascination about assassins is that one can actually observe the alteration of history, just so long as the victim is famous and important, or becomes, for example, the spark that can ignite a European war. But there is something specious in this. President Kennedy may have indicated his belief in Civil Rights, but it was his successor Lyndon Johnson who saw fit to make the necessary laws. Kennedy did indeed stand firm over USSR missiles going to Cuba, but he also put in train one of the most comprehensive build-ups of the arms trade this century. So far as the American economy was concerned, nothing was more profitable than the 'threat' of the Cold War, and the immediate need to lay siege to North Vietnam. As the Vietnam war machine boomed, it was no coincidence that the Russians beefed up their nuclear strike capabilities in South East Asia. Thus the Kennedy regime was merely a decorative cosmetic to the war machine that led us so fatly through the Sixties. And a Presidential death altered none of this progress. That day in Dallas couldn't possibly have changed history.

But what is it that so many of us found compelling about this public death? It can't simply be put down to a love of the conspiracy theory, though there has never been any shortage of this. Over the years it has become a regular industry. Cuban exiles and mafia barons planned it in a deadly alliance of interests. Dallas police officers and Texas oil billionaires fitted up the poor sap Oswald right from the start. Lyndon Johnson was the acceptable President because he wasn't interested in harassing drugs-and-extortion rackets from coast to coast. In the final weeks leading up to the assassination, there were two Oswalds, not one; a shadow Oswald, a look-alike, acquired guns and an unusually high public profile in various pro-Castro groups. Tippit and Ruby and Oswald all belonged to an underworld of gay club activity, they were on FBI files, and they could be hired to clean up after the assassination. Or there is the theory, held to firmly in some quarters, that . . .

And you take a deep breath and sigh. Why are so many people determined to fill this vacuum? We possess an encyclopedia of detail about this subject but it remains irritating that nothing is properly labelled *guilty*. As if we cannot tolerate the idea of a world without blame.

Of course, any suggestion that Oswald fired alongside others, or that he was used as a fall-guy by others, immediately turns the Warren Report on its head. Beside this is the curious fear that – just as the Nazis were determined to pin the 1933 burning of the Reichstag building on one Dutch Communist, Marinus van der Lubbe – certain interests needed to pin everything about that day in Dallas, 1963, on Lee Harvey Oswald. Why?

I like to think that American government agent at the London Embassy got closest to the nub of the problem. However you approach this mystery, dismay and doubt still linger on. And yet we are only left with this man Oswald; no credible new suspect has been found. The range of writers attracted to this story is surprisingly catholic: there have been barristers, history professors, SF buffs, novelists, and even a former President of the United States. But all we have is the supposed promise of Jack Kennedy and a charmed family. All we glimpse is this sallow young Oswald with his twitched mouth and darty, glittering eyes, and the few words he spoke on TV – 'Nobody has accused me of anything, sir', and 'No, sir, I have not been arrested for killing the President', and finally, more poignantly, 'They will not allow me to speak to a lawyer. I got these bruises on my head in back of the police cells, sir.' Hours later he was shot dead. Within a few days his young Russian widow, Marina, started to prime reporters with her account of her husband. And for a time it seemed her very soul was held in the safekeeping of the FBI. Crass it may be to discover the riddle of Oswald has overtaken all interest in the fate of Jack Kennedy. But the riddle intrigues, and if there is one thing all the writers share in common, it is the sense that you are dealing with something very intelligent.

However you look at Kennedy, Tippit, Oswald and Ruby, you come across a series of incidents which could only be put together by serious, intelligent leg-work. The probabilities of guilt are continually massaged by intricate and often too convenient pieces of circumstantial evidence. Half of what we need to know is missing and the other half is ground into dust by more questions than have answers. Thus this riddle will nag on into perpetuity. It has become an irritant, a piece of grit inside the human oyster.

At that juncture I realized I had to step aside from the quest for a logical answer. Instead of detailing the facts, I wanted to understand the nature of the events.

Lee Harvey Oswald: a far mean streak of indepence brought on by negleck does not try to apportion blame. Theories – conspiratorial or otherwise – were put aside. The play attempts to look closely at the enigmatic Oswald. Give him some living verisimilitude. What I believe emerges from this is a portrait of a man who quintessentially could never have done anything on his own. If Maries are dreamers and Marthas are doers, Lee Oswald clearly emerges as one of life's Maries. Whatever else an audience might take away from this play is up to them. They can leave conjuring up any number of outlandish theories. They are welcome to all the irritant grits in the human oyster they can cope with. But for the time being, Lee Oswald is all we have. And that violent hour in Dallas. And perhaps a hint that there remains something else. It is a curious thing. It is something intelligent, perhaps malign, and yet quite elusive, and it takes the shape of barely discernible *presences* behind all the facts. *Presences* you will invariably come up against whenever you scrutinize the Warren Report, and not even two million words can exorcize them. Like ghosts in history, notable only for their absence, they have left the merest traces of their actions behind, the faintest spoors, as of intelligent preparations and precisely laid plans quite unaccountably gone awry, panic and hasty second measures, followed then perhaps by sudden flight.

MICHAEL HASTINGS
Brixton, 1989

THE EMPEROR

by Michael Hastings and Jonathan Miller

Author's Note

Part of my enthusiasm for the quality of Ryszard Kapuściński's *The Emperor* is inspired by the excellence of the translation from the Polish by William R. Brand and Katarzyna Mroczkowska-Brand. They have also translated two other books by Kapuściński, *Shah of Shahs* and *Another Day of Life*.

M.H.

The riddle of the white ant is that – unladen it will not risk its life to jump the impossible gorge. But laden – it doesn't hesitate.

Eugene Marais, *The Soul of the White Ant*

CHARACTERS

UND
FOST
HULET
ARAT
AMSET

★

N.B. Und, Hulet, Fost, Arat and Amset are the
transliterated Amharic for numbers one to five.
Each character represents various and many in-
dividual voices from the book. It is a choral
piece.

The Emperor, directed by Jonathan Miller in association with Michael Hastings, was first performed at the Theatre Upstairs, Royal Court Theatre, on 17 March 1987, with the following cast:

UND	Ben Onwukwe
HULET	Nabil Shaban
ARAT	Hepburn Graham
AMSET	Okon Jones
FOST	Stefan Kalipha
DESIGNER	Richard Hudson
LIGHTING DESIGNER	Ace McCarron

The play re-opened on the main stage at the Royal Court Theatre, with the same cast, on 3 September 1987.

A televised version of this production, directed by Jonathan Miller, based on the Hastings / Miller play and with the same cast, was shown on BBC2 TV in January 1988.

Throughout the three rehearsal periods the company contributed much to the overall design of the production; especially Hepburn Graham and stage manager Thomas Betteridge, who restaged the original production in September 1987.

ACT ONE

We dramatize a chiaroscuro of airs and savage obedience. In the old palace arboreal cornices collect dust and breath hovers along the corridor. Groomed lawns recline in the sun beneath the sprinklers. The leopards are patient.

There are a number of doors. One set of three imperial doors open on to each other in a narrow file. There is a swing door at waist level. There are a number of box-like surprise doors large enough for heads and shoulders. There is a cat-flap door at the base of an Imperial door. A single trap for a neck is on the ground. Some doors open on to a perspective of doors. Other doors reveal darknesses. A window is blocked with brickwork.

The top half of one door conceals a cupboard which is stuffed with Imperial cushions. During the interval this cupboard is removed and a blood bag fitted to the back of the upper half of the door.

There is a cuckoo clock. One door is raised from the ground.

UND *steps out of the shadows, wreathed in dark mist. He wears a plain dark suit.*

UND: Of course I remember. Wasn't it just yesterday? Yesterday, but a century ago. In this city, but on a planet that is now far away. How all these things get confused. Times, places, the world broken in pieces, not to be glued back together again. Only the memory – that's the only remnant of life.
(*Leaves.* HULET *scuttles out of the swing door, carrying a satin kerchief.*)
HULET: It was a small dog, a Japanese breed. His name was Lulu. He was allowed to sleep in the Emperor's great bed. During various ceremonies, he would run away from the Emperor's lap and pee on dignitaries' shoes. The august gentlemen were not allowed to flinch or make the slightest gesture when they

felt their feet getting wet. I had to move among the dignitaries and wipe the urine from their shoes with a satin cloth. This was my job for ten years.

(HULET *wipes a person's shoe, and leaves. He dabs his face, too.* FOST *emerges. Plain suit.*)

FOST: The Emperor slept in a roomy bed made of light walnut. He was so slight and frail that you couldn't see him – he was lost among the sheets. In old age he became even smaller. He weighed fifty kilograms.

(ARAT *is at a door. Grey suit.*)

ARAT: Fifty-two.

FOST: He ate less and less, and he never drank alcohol. His knees stiffened up, and when he was tired he dragged his feet, swaying from side to side as if on stilts. But when he knew that someone was watching him, he forced a certain elasticity into his muscles, with great effort, so that he moved with dignity and his imperial silhouette remained ramrod straight. Each step was a struggle between shuffling and dignity, between leaning and the vertical line. His Majesty never forgot about this infirmity of his old age, which he did not want to reveal lest it weaken the prestige and solemnity of the King of Kings.

ARAT: But we servants of the royal bedchamber, who saw his unguarded moments, knew how much the effort cost him. He had the habit of sleeping little and rising early, when it was still dark outside. He treated sleep as a dire necessity that purposelessly robbed him of time he would rather have spent ruling or at Imperial functions. Sleep was a private, intimate interval in his life meant to be passed amid decorations and lights.

(AMSET *enters. Plain suit.*)

AMSET: Let me add, however, that the Emperor never showed the slightest sign of irritation, nervousness, anger, rage or frustration. It seemed that he never knew such states, that his nerves were cold and dead like steel, or that he had no nerves at all. It was an inborn characteristic that His Highness knew how to develop and perfect, following the principle that in politics nervousness signifies a weakness that encourages opponents and emboldens subordinates to make secret jokes. His Majesty knew that a joke is a dangerous form of opposition and he kept his psyche in perfect order.

FOST: He got up at four or five, and when going abroad on a visit, at three in the morning. Upon waking, he rang the buzzer on his night-stand – the vigilant servants were waiting for the sound. The lights were turned on in the Palace. It was a signal to the Empire that His Supreme Majesty had begun a new day.

UND: The Emperor began his day by listening to informers' reports. The night breeds dangerous conspiracies, and he knew that what happens at night is more important than what happens during the day.

AMSET: The custom of relating things by word of mouth had this advantage: if need be, the Emperor could say that a given dignitary had told him something quite different from what had really been said, and the latter could not defend himself, having no written proof. Thus the Emperor heard from his subordinates not what they told him but what he thought should be said. His Venerable Highness had his ideas, and he would adjust to them all the signals that came from his surroundings. It was the same with writing, for our monarch not only never used his ability to read, but rumour has it he never wrote anything and never signed anything in his own hand. Though he ruled for half a century, not even those closest to him know what his signature looked like.

(HULET *pulls* FOST*'s head close to his.* FOST *writes.*)

HULET: During the Emperor's hours of official function, the Minister of the Pen always stood at hand and took down all the Emperor's orders and instructions. His Majesty spoke very softly, barely moving his lips. The Minister of the Pen, standing half a step from the throne, had to bend his ear close to the Imperial lips in order to hear and write down the Imperial decisions. Furthermore, the Emperor's words were usually unclear and ambiguous, especially when he did not want to take a definite stand on a matter that required his opinion. One had to admire the Emperor's dexterity. When asked by a dignitary for the Imperial decision, he would not answer straight out, but would rather speak in a voice so quiet that it reached only the Minister of the Pen, who moved his ear as close as a microphone. The Minister transcribed his ruler's scant and foggy mutterings. All the rest was interpretation, and that was a matter for the Minister, who passed down the decision in writing.

(HULET *ceases being the Emperor.*)

FOST: The Minister of the Pen was the Emperor's closest confidant and enjoyed enormous power. From the secret cabbala of the monarch's words he could construct any decision that he wished. If a move by the Emperor dazzled everyone with its accuracy and wisdom, it was one more proof that God's Chosen One was infallible.

(FOST *ceases being the Minister of the Pen. Joins* HULET *and* ARAT *and* UND *as a group of ministers.*)

AMSET: On the other hand, if from some corner the breeze carried rumours of discontent to the monarch's ear, he could blame it all on

ALL: the Minister's stupidity.

AMSET: And so the Minister was the most hated personality of the court. Public opinion, convinced of His Venerable Highness's wisdom and goodness, blamed the Minister for any thoughtless or malicious decisions.

SOME: Of which there were many. True.

ALL: True.

AMSET: But in the Palace questions were always asked from top to bottom, and never vice versa. When the first question was asked in a direction opposite to the customary one, it was a signal that the revolution had begun.

(UND *wants to interrupt. Plain suit.*)

UND: But we're getting ahead of ourselves and must go back to the moment when the Emperor appears –

AMSET: (*Faint*) Of course.

UND: – on the Palace steps in the morning and sets out for his early walk. He enters the park.

(FOST *becomes the Emperor.* AMSET *whispers to him.*)

Solomon Kedir, the head of the Palace spies, approaches and gives his report. The Emperor walks along the avenue and

Kedir stays a step behind him, talking all the while. Who met whom, where, and what they talked about.

ARAT: Against whom they are forming alliances.

HULET: Whether or not one could call it a conspiracy.

(FOST *breaks away.* UND *becomes the Emperor.*)

FOST: This department, part of Kedir's office, decodes the communications that pass among the divisions – it's good to be sure that no subversive thoughts are hatching there. His Distinguished Highness asks no questions, makes no comments. He walks and listens. Sometimes he stops before the lions' cage to throw them a leg of veal that a servant has handed to him. He watches the lions' rapacity and smiles.

ARAT: Then he approaches the leopards, which are chained, and gives them ribs of beef. His Majesty has to be careful as he approaches the unpredictable beasts of prey. Finally he moves on, with Kedir behind continuing his report.

(UND *and* AMSET *and* ARAT *freeze for a moment.* ARAT *becomes the Emperor. He leans beside a secret box. The box snaps open and* AMSET *whispers.*)

ARAT: At a certain moment His Highness bows his head, which is a signal for Kedir to move away. He bows and disappears down the avenue, never turning his back on the Emperor. At this moment the waiting Minister of Industry and Commerce, Makonen Habte-Wald, emerges from behind a tree. He falls in, a step behind the Emperor, and delivers his report.

AMSET: Makonen Habte-Wald keeps his own network of informers, both to satisfy a consuming passion for intrigue and to ingratiate himself with His Venerable Highness. On the basis of his information, he now briefs the Emperor on what happened last night. Again, His Majesty walks on, listening without questions or comments, keeping his hands behind his back. He approaches a flock of flamingoes, but the shy birds scatter when he comes near. The Emperor smiles at the sight of creatures that refuse to obey him. At last, still walking, he nods his head. Habte-Wald falls silent and retreats backwards, disappearing down the avenue.

(HULET *indicates the movement of flamingoes. Plain suit.* ARAT *steps back.* AMSET *and* UND *and* FOST *leave.* HULET *scuttles into a corner.*)

ARAT: Next, as if springing up from the ground, rises the hunched silhouette of the devoted confidant Asha Walde-Mikael. This dignitary supervises the government political police. He competes with Solomon Kedir's intelligence service and battles fiercely against private informer networks like the one that Makonen Habte-Wald has at his disposal.

HULET: The occupation to which these people devoted themselves was hard and dangerous. They lived in fear of not reporting something in time and falling into disgrace, or of a competitor's reporting it better so that the Emperor would think:

(UND *and* FOST *and* AMSET *and* ARAT *appear in sequence in small box doors.*)

UND: Why did Solomon give me a feast today and Makonen only bring me left-overs?

FOST: Did he say nothing because he didn't know?

AMSET: Or did he hold his tongue because he belongs to the conspiracy?

ARAT: Hadn't I often experienced, at cost to myself, betrayal by my most trusted allies?

(UND *steps forward. The doors snap shut.*)

UND: The Emperor punished silence.

(AMSET *enters.*)

AMSET: On the other hand, incoherent streams of words tired and irritated the Imperial ear, so nervous loquaciousness was also a poor solution. Even the way these people looked told of the threat under which they lived. Tired, looking as if they hadn't slept, they acted under feverish stress, pursuing their victims in the stale air of hatred and fear that surrounded them all. They had no shield but the Emperor, and the Emperor could undo them with one wave of his hand. No, His Benevolent Majesty did not make their lives easy.

UND: As I've mentioned, the Emperor never commented on or questioned the reports he received during his morning walks, about the state of conspiracy in the Empire. But he knew what he was doing, as I shall show you.

(FOST *enters*.)

FOST: His Highness wanted to receive the reports in a pure state, because if he asked questions or expressed opinions the informant would obligingly adjust his report to meet the Emperor's expectations. Then the whole system of informing would collapse into subjectivity and fall prey to anyone's wilfulness. The monarch would not know what was going on in the country and the Palace.

(FOST *becomes the Emperor*. HULET *illustrates the movements of an ant-eater*.)

ARAT: Finishing his walk, the Emperor listens to what was reported last night by Asha's people. He feeds the dogs and the black panther, and then he admires the ant-eater that he recently received as a gift from the President of Uganda. He nods his head and Asha walks away, bent over, wondering whether he said more or less than what was reported by his most fervent enemies.

(AMSET *and* UND *retreat as if in fear*.)

AMSET: Solomon, the enemy of Makonen and Asha.

UND: Makonen, the enemy of Asha and Solomon.

HULET: And so the Emperor finishes his walk alone. It grows light in the park, the fog thins out, and reflected sunlight glimmers on the lawns. The Emperor ponders. Now is the time to lay out strategies and tactics, to solve the puzzles of personality, to plan his next move on the chessboard of power. He thinks deeply about what was contained in the informants' reports.

(FOST *ponders by the door. Leaves*. AMSET *is hiding behind a corner, giggling*.)

AMSET: Little of importance; they usually report on each other. His Majesty has made mental notes of everything. His mind is a computer that retains every detail, even the smallest datum will be remembered. There was no personnel office in the Palace, no dossiers full of personal information. All this the Emperor carried in his mind, all the most important files about the elite. I see him now as he walks, stops, walks again, lifts his head upward as though absorbed in prayer. Oh God, save me from those who, crawling on their knees, hide a knife that they would like to sink into my back. But how can God help? All the people surrounding the Emperor are just like that – on their knees, and with knives. It's never comfortable on the summits.

(FOST *makes a grand entrance through the sets of double doors*.)

FOST: As the keeper of the third door, I was the most important footman in the Audience Hall. The Hall had three sets of doors, and three footmen to open and close them, but I held the highest rank because the Emperor passed through my door. When His Most Exalted Majesty left the room, it was I who opened the door. It was an art to open the door at the right moment, the exact instant. To open the door too early would have been reprehensible, as if I were hurrying the Emperor out. If I opened it too late, on the other hand, His Sublime Highness would have to slow down, or perhaps even stop, which would detract from his lordly dignity, a dignity that meant getting around without collisions or obstacles.

(FOST *demonstrates how to open the doors.* ARAT *is there. Steps forward imperiously.* FOST *trembles.* FOST *leaves*.)

ARAT: Our office was in the Old Palace, where most of the Imperial institutions were located, since the Emperor wanted to have everything within easy reach. He was brought there in one of the twenty-seven automobiles that made up his private fleet. He liked automobiles. He prized the Rolls-Royces for their dignified lines, but for a change he would also use the Mercedes-Benzes and the Lincoln Continentals. I'll remind you that our Emperor brought the first cars into Ethiopia, and he was always well disposed towards the exponents of technical progress, whom unfortunately our traditional nation always disliked.

(AMSET *enters*.)

AMSET: Didn't our Emperor almost lose his power, and his life, when he brought the first airplane from Europe in the Twenties? The simple airplane struck people as an invention of Satan and in the courts of magnates there sprung up conspiracies against the Emperor as if he were a cabbalist or a necromancer. His Revered Highness had to control ever more carefully his inclinations to act the pioneer until, in that stage of life when novelty holds little interest for an aged man, he almost gave them up.

ARAT: And so at nine o'clock he would arrive at the Old Palace. Before the gate a crowd of subjects waited to try to hand petitions to the Emperor.

(UND *and* FOST *and* ARAT *and* AMSET *and* HULET *move to line up.*)

UND: Because our nation is illiterate, and justice is usually sought by the poor, people would go into debt for years to pay a clerk to write down their complaints and demands.

FOST: There was also a problem of protocol, since custom required the humblest ones to kneel before the Emperor with their faces to the ground. How can anyone hand an envelope to a passing limousine from that posture? The problem was solved in the following manner. The vehicle would slow, the benevolent face of the monarch would appear behind the glass, and the security people from the next car would take some of the envelopes from the extended hands of the populace.

(UND *and* FOST *and* ARAT *and* AMSET *push the crowd back.*)

HULET: Only some, for there was a whole thicket of these hands. If the mob crawled too close to the oncoming cars, the guards had to push back and the solemnity of majesty required that the procession be smooth and free of unexpected delays.

UND: Now the vehicles drove up the ascending avenue and stopped in the Palace courtyard. Here too a crowd awaited the Emperor, but a different one from the rabble that had been furiously driven away by the select members of the Imperial Bodyguard. Those waiting in the courtyard to greet the Emperor were from the monarch's own circles.

ARAT: We gathered early so as not to miss the Emperor's arrival, because that moment had a special significance for us.

HULET: Everyone wanted very badly to be noted by the Emperor.

(*All jostle and push and try to gain ground.*)

AMSET: No, one didn't dream of special notice, with the Revered Emperor catching sight of you, coming up, and starting a conversation. No –

ALL: (*Intensely whisper*) No no . . .

AMSET: – nothing like that, I assure you. One wanted only the smallest, second-rate sort of attention, nothing that burdened the Emperor with any obligations. A passing notice –

ALL: (*Jostling and shoving*) Yes yes . . .

AMSET: – a fraction of a second, yet the sort of notice that later would make one tremble inside and overwhelm one with the triumphal thought –

ALL: (*Sigh*) 'I have been noticed.'

UND: What strength it gave afterwards! What unlimited possibilities it created! Let's say that the Imperial gaze just grazes –

ALL: Grazes . . .

UND: – your face – just grazes! You could say that it was really nothing, but on the other hand, how could it really be nothing, when it did graze you? Immediately you feel the temperature of your face rise, and the blood rush to your head, and your heart beat harder.

HULET: These are the best proofs that the eye of the Protector has touched you, but so what? These proofs are of no importance at the moment. More important is the process that might have taken place in His Majesty's memory. You see, it was known that His Majesty, not using his powers of reading and writing, had a phenomenally developed visual memory. On this gift of nature the owner of the face over which the Imperial gaze had passed could build his hopes. Because he could already count on some passing trace, even an indistinct trace, having imprinted itself in His Highness's memory.

ARAT: Now, you had to manoeuvre in the crowd with such perseverance and determination, so squeeze yourself and worm through, so push, so jostle, so position your face, dispose and manipulate it in such a way, that the Emperor's glance, unwillingly and unknowingly, would notice, notice, notice. Then you waited for the moment to come when the Emperor would think:

(AMSET *breaks away from the heaving crowd, and becomes the Emperor.*)

AMSET: 'Just a minute, I know the face, but I don't know the name.'

(ARAT *breaks away from the crowd, and the grabbing hands.*)

ARAT: And let's say he would ask for the name. Only the name, but that's enough! Now the face and the name are joined, and a person comes into being, a ready candidate for nomination. Because the face alone – that's anonymous. The name alone – an abstraction. You have to materialize yourself, take on shape and form, gain distinctness.

(FOST *breaks away, too.*)

FOST: Oh, that was the good fortune most longed for, but how difficult it was to realize! Because in the courtyard where the Emperor's retinue awaited him, there were tens, no I say it without exaggeration, hundreds eager to push their faces forward. Face rubbed against face, the taller ones squelching down the shorter ones, the darker ones overshadowing the lighter ones.

(*They regroup and become a pulsing magma.*)

ALL: Face despised face, face, face.

UND: The older ones moving in front of the younger ones, the weaker ones giving way to the stronger ones.

HULET: The common ones clashing with the noble ones, the grasping ones against the weaklings.

AMSET: Face crushed face, but even the humiliated ones, the ones pushed away, the third-rates and the defeated ones, even those – from a certain distance imposed by the law of hierarchy, it's true – still moved towards the front, showing here and there from behind the first-rate, titled ones, if only as fragments: an ear, a piece of temple, a cheek or a jaw . . . just to be closer to the Emperor's eye!

(*They heave and push and slowly collapse. They break away. They leave.* HULET *remains.*)

HULET: If His Benevolent Majesty wanted to capture with his glance the whole scene that opened before him when he stepped from his car, he would perceive that not only was a hundred-faced magma, at once humble and frenetic, rolling towards him, but also that, aside from the central, highly titled group, to the right and left, in front of him and behind him, far and even farther away, in the doors and in the windows and on the paths, whole multitudes of lackeys, kitchen servants, janitors, gardeners, and policemen were pushing their faces forward to be noticed.

(UND *waves from a cat-flap door,* ARAT *from a secret box,* AMSET *from a doorway,* FOST *from an impossibly contorted corner. All waving.* HULET *scuttles into a corner.* AMSET *stays in his doorway. Emerges.*)

AMSET: And His Majesty takes it all in. Does it surprise or amaze him? I doubt it. His Majesty himself was once a part of the hundred-faced magma. Didn't he have to push his face forward in order to become heir to the throne at the age of only twenty-four? And he had a hell of a lot of competition! A whole squadron of experienced notables was striving for the crown. But they were in a hurry, one cutting in front of the other, at each other's throats, trembling, impatient. Quickly, quickly, to the throne! His Peerless Majesty knew how to wait. And that is an all-important ability. Without that ability to wait, to realize humbly that the chance may come only after years of waiting, there is no politician.

(AMSET *leaves.*)

UND: His Distinguished Majesty waited for ten years to become the heir to the throne, and then fourteen more years to become Emperor. In all, close to a quarter of a century of cautious but energetic striving for the crown. I say 'cautious' because it was characteristic of His Majesty to be secretive, discreet, and silent. He knew the Palace. He knew that every wall had ears and that from behind every arras gazed eyes attentively scrutinizing him. So he had to be cunning and shrewd. First of all, one can't unmask oneself too early, showing the rapacity for power, because that galvanizes competitors, making them rise to combat. They will strike and destroy the one who has moved to the fore. No, one should walk in step for years, making sure not to spring ahead, waiting attentively for the right moment. In 1930 this game brought His Majesty the crown, which he kept for forty-four years.

(HULET *bears forth a fine cushion.*)

HULET: I was His Most Virtuous Highness's pillow-bearer for twenty-six years. His Majesty spent the hour between nine and ten in the morning handing out assignments in the Audience Hall, and thus this time was called the Hour of Assignments. The Emperor would enter the Hall, where a row of waiting dignitaries, nominated for assignment, bowed humbly. His Majesty would take his place on the throne, and when he had seated himself I would slide a pillow under his feet. This had to be done like lightning so as not to leave Our Distinguished Monarch's legs hanging in the air for even a moment. We all know that His Highness was of small stature. At the same time, the dignity of the Imperial Office required that he be elevated above his subjects, even in a strictly physical sense. Thus the Imperial thrones had long legs and high seats, especially those left by Emperor Menelik, an exceptionally tall man. Therefore a contradiction arose between the necessity of a high throne and the figure of His Venerable Majesty, a contradiction most sensitive and troublesome precisely in the region of the legs, since it is difficult to imagine that an appropriate dignity can be maintained by a person whose legs are dangling in the air like those of a small child. The pillow solved this delicate and all-important conundrum. His Majesty could not go anywhere without me, since his dignity required that he always take his place on a throne, and he could not sit on a throne without a pillow, and I was the pillow-bearer. I had mastered (ARAT *steps forward carrying a decrepit royal chair.* HULET *tosses the cushion in front of the chair. Places it carefully.* UND *steps forward and sits regally.* HULET *glows.*) the special protocol of this speciality, and even possessed an extremely useful, expert knowledge: the height of various thrones. This allowed me quickly to choose a pillow of just the right size, so that a shocking ill fit, allowing a gap to appear between the pillow and the Emperor's shoes, would not occur. In my storeroom I had fifty-two (HULET *shows us the cupboard in the upper part of the door. He reaches to open it. A cascade of pillows tumbles out over him. He squeals, then pulls himself together.* AMSET *has taken off his jacket.*

He wears braces. He tries to tidy up the cushions and close the offending cupboard door.)

pillows of various sizes, thicknesses, materials and colours. I personally monitored their storage constantly so that fleas – fleas – the plague of our country – would not breed there, since the consequences of any such oversight could lead to a very unpleasant scandal!

(HULET *explores his body for fleas.* FOST *makes another flourishing entrance.*)

FOST: The Hour of Assignments set the whole Palace trembling!

ARAT: Working as a protocol official in the Hall of Audiences, I noticed that, in general, assignment caused very basic physical changes in a man. This so fascinated me that I started to watch more closely. First, the whole figure of a man changes. What had been slender and trim-waisted now starts to become a square silhouette. It is a massive and solemn square: a symbol of the solemnity and weight of power. We can already see that this is not just anybody's silhouette, but that of visible dignity and responsibility. A slowing-down of movements accompanies this change in the figure. A man who has been singled out by His Distinguished Majesty will not jump, run, frolic, or cut a caper.

(FOST *adopts a suitable pose.* AMSET *moves into an obedient self.* UND *leans precariously. All grin.* ARAT *takes us around the statues.*)

ARAT: No. His step is solemn: he sets his feet firmly on the ground, bending his body slightly forward to show his determination to push through adversity, ordering precisely the movement of his hands so as to avoid nervous, disorganized gesticulation. Furthermore, the facial features become solemn, almost stiffened, more worried and closed, but still capable of a momentary change to optimism or approval. All in all, however, they are set so as to create no possibility of psychological contact. One cannot relax, rest, or catch one's breath next to such a face. The gaze changes too: its length and angle are altered. The gaze is trained on a completely unattainable point. In accordance with the laws of optics, an appointee cannot perceive us when we talk to him, since his focal point is well beyond us. We cannot be perceived because he looks obliquely, and, by a strange periscopic principle, even the shortest appointees look over our heads towards an unfathomable distance or in the direction of some particular, private thought. We realize that an attempt to convey our own thoughts would be senseless and petty. Therefore we fall silent.

(*They pause in silence. Break away.*)

UND: The degree of power wielded by those in the Palace corresponded not to the hierarchy of positions, but rather to the frequency of access to His Worthy Majesty. That was our situation in the Palace. It was said that one was important if one had the Emperor's ear more often. More often, and for longer. For that ear the lobbies fought their fiercest battles; the ear was the highest prize in the game. It was enough, though it was not easy, to get close to the all-powerful ear and whisper. Whisper, that's all. Get it in, let it stay there, if only as a floating impression, a tiny seed.

(AMSET *becomes the Emperor.* ARAT *and* FOST *and* HULET *surround him, whispering.* HULET *seems to have some difficulty reaching up for the Emperor's ear. In desperation he hugs close and tries to aim conversation somewhere around the Emperor's knees.*)

UND: The time will come when the impression solidifies, the seed grows. Then we will gather the harvest. These were subtle manoeuvres, demanding tact, because His Majesty, despite amazingly indefatigable energy and perseverance, was a human being with an ear that one could not overload and stuff up without causing irritation and an angry reaction. That's why access was limited and the fight for a piece of the Emperor's ear never stopped. I will add that, in relation to his modest size and pleasing form, His Supreme Majesty had ears of a large configuration.

(*The appellants break off.* ARAT *tries a flourish.*)

ARAT: And so, having finished the Hour of Assignments, His Indefatigable Majesty would move on to the Golden Hall.

(UND *and* FOST *begin to direct the rabble down below.*)

AMSET: Here began the Hour of the Cash-box. This hour came between ten and eleven in the morning. His Highness was accompanied by the saintly Aba Hanna, who in turn was assisted by his faithful bag-bearer. Someone with good ears and a good nose could tell how the Palace rustled with money, smelled of it. But this called for special imagination and sensitivity, because money was not lying around the chambers, and His Merciful Highness had no inclination to spread packets of dollars among his favourites. No, His Highness cared little for that sort of thing.

(AMSET *pushes aside* UND *and* FOST.)

Even though, dear friend, it might seem incomprehensible to you, not even Aba Hanna's little bag was a bottomless treasury. The masters of ceremony had to use all sorts of stratagems to prevent the Emperor from being embarrassed financially. I remember, for instance, how His Majesty paid the salaries of foreign engineers but showed no inclination to pay our own masons after the construction of the new Imperial Palace. These simple masons gathered in front of the Palace they had built and began asking for what was due them. The Supreme Master of Palace Ceremony appeared on the balcony and asked them to move to the rear of the Palace, where His Magnanimous Highness would shower them with money. The delighted crowd went round the back to the indicated spot – which enabled His Supreme Majesty to leave unembarrassed through the front door and go to the Old Palace, where the court awaited him.

(HULET *becomes the Emperor.* FOST *and* ARAT *stand behind him.*)

FOST: I was the purse-bearer to Aba Hanna Jema, the God-fearing confessor and treasurer to the Emperor. Aba Hanna's un-limited access to the throne proved the intimacy of this relationship. You could even call it continuous access. As keeper of the cash-box and confessor to our much-lamented monarch, Aba could look into the Imperial soul and the Imperial pocket – in other words he could see the Imperial person in its dignified entirety. As his purse-bearer, I always accompanied Aba in his fiscal activities, carrying behind him the bag of top-grade lambskin that those who destroyed everything later exhibited in the streets. I also took care of another bag, a large one that was filled with small coins on the eve of national holidays: the Emperor's birthday, the anniversary of his coronation, and the anniversary of his return from exile. On such occasions our august ruler went to the most crowded and lively quarter of Addis Ababa, where on a specially constructed platform I would place the heavy, jingling bag from which His Benevolent Majesty would scoop the handfuls of coppers that he threw into the crowd of beggars and other such greedy riff-raff. The rapacious mob would create such a hubbub, however, that this charitable action always had to end in a shower of police batons against the heads of the frenzied, pushy rabble. Saddened, His Highness would have to walk away from the platform. Often he was unable to empty even half the bag.

(HULET *and* FOST *and* UND *break away.* AMSET *stands by a door. The others circle around him pushing for attention. They become courtiers. They march as dignitaries. They run as messengers. They grovel as honours are bestowed.*)

AMSET: At the other end of the Hall people are crowding in, apparently without order, but everyone remembers his place in the line. I can call it a crowd, since His Gracious Majesty received an endless number of subjects every day. When he stayed in Addis Ababa the Palace overflowed. It pulsated with exuberant life – though, naturally, a hierarchy was to be found here as well – rows of cars flowed through the courtyard, delegations crowded the corridors, ambassadors chatted in the antechambers, masters of ceremony rushed around with feverish eyes, the guard changed, messengers ran in with piles of papers, ministers dropped by, simply and modestly, like ordinary people. Hundreds of subjects tried to wangle their petitions or denunciations into the hands of the dignitaries. One could see the general staff, members of the Crown Council, managers of Imperial estates, deputies – in other words an excited and exhilarated crowd.

(*The courtiers fade away like blown dust.*)

All this would disappear in an instant when His Distinguished Majesty would leave the capital on a visit abroad or to some province to lay a cornerstone, open a new road, or find out about the troubles of the people in order to encourage or console them. The Palace would immediately become empty and change into a replica of itself, a prop. The Palace servants did their laundry and strung their wash on clotheslines, the Palace children grazed their goats on the lawns, the masters of ceremony hung out in local bars, the guards would chain the gates shut and sleep under the trees. Then His Majesty would return, the fanfares would sound, and the Palace would come to life again.

(UND *sits on the chair.* FOST *and* ARAT *and* AMSET *and* HULET *step forth.* FOST *has a large cream parasol.* HULET *becomes the Emperor.* FOST *and* AMSET *and* ARAT *take turns to spin the parasol as they circle around the Emperor, begging favours.*)

UND: In the Golden Hall there was always electricity in the air. One could feel the current flowing through the temples of those who had been summoned, making them quiver. Everyone knew the source of that current: the little bag of finest lambskin. People would approach His Benevolent Highness by turns, saying why they needed money. His Majesty would listen and ask questions. Here I must admit that His Highness was most meticulous about financial matters. Any expenditure, anywhere in the Empire, of more than ten dollars required his personal approval, and if a minister came to ask approval for spending only one dollar, he would be praised. To repair a minister's car – the Emperor's approval is needed. To replace a leaking pipe in the city – the Emperor's approval is needed. To buy sheets for a hotel – the Emperor must approve it.

(*They stop rotating beneath the fast parasol.* ARAT *breaks away.* UND *crawls to the Emperor's feet.*)

ARAT: How you should admire, my friend, the diligent thrift of His August Majesty, who spent most of his royal time checking accounts, listening to cost estimates, rejecting proposals, and brooding over human greed, cunning and meddling. His lively curiosity, vigilance, and exemplary economy always attracted mention. He had a fiscal bent, and his Minister of Finance was counted among those with the most access to the Emperor. Yet to those in need His

Highness would stretch out a generous hand. Having listened as his questions were answered, His Charitable Majesty would inform the petitioner that his financial needs would be met. The delighted subject would make the deepest bow.

(UND *crawls backward with the gift in his hand. Crawling and waving and bobbing, he exits.*)

His Magnanimous Highness would then turn his head in the direction of Aba Hanna and specify in a whisper the sum of money that the saintly nobleman was to take from the purse. Aba Hanna would plunge his hand into the bag, take out the money, put it into an envelope and hand it to the lucky recipient. Bow after bow, backward, backward, shuffling his feet and stumbling, the fortunate one would leave.

(UND *gives a woeful moan off-stage.* HULET *breaks away.*)

HULET: And afterwards, one could unfortunately hear the cries of the wretched ingrate. Because in the envelope he would find only a fraction of the sum that – as the insatiable thieves always swore – had been promised to him by our generous Emperor.

(FOST *breaks away and gently binds the parasol.* HULET *crawls after him imploring like a beggar.*)

FOST: Have you any idea what money means in a poor country? Money in a poor country and money in a rich country are two different things. In a rich country, money is a piece of paper with which you buy goods on the market. You are only a customer. Even a millionaire is only a customer. He may purchase more, but he remains a customer, nothing more. And in a poor country? In a poor country, money is a wonderful, thick hedge, dazzling and always blooming, which separates you from everything else. Through that hedge you do not see creeping poverty, you do not smell the stench of misery, and you do not hear the voices of the human dregs. But at the same time you know that all of that exists, and you feel proud because of your hedge. You have money; that means you have wings. You are the bird of paradise that everyone admires.

(HULET *chases after* FOST. FOST *doesn't see him.* HULET *tugs at his legs.* FOST *reluctantly tosses him a coin. They leave.* AMSET *and* ARAT *are alone on the stage.*)

AMSET: Though everyone – if he proved his loyalty – could count on a bountiful gift, there were still continuous quarrels between lobbies, constant struggles for privileges, incessant grabbing, and all because of the needs of that bird of paradise that fills every man. His Most Extraordinary Majesty liked to watch this elbowing. He liked the people of the court to multiply their belongings, he liked their accounts to grow and their purses to swell. I don't remember His Magnanimous Highness's ever demoting someone and pressing his head to the cobblestones because of corruption.

ARAT: One case, though, was different. An outstanding patriot and a leader of the partisans in the war against Mussolini, Tekele Wolda Hawariat by name, was ill-disposed towards the Emperor. He refused special privileges, never showed any inclination to corruption. His Charitable Majesty had him imprisoned for many years, and then cut his head off.

(ARAT *studies* AMSET. AMSET *remembers.* HULET *scuttles back, looking proud.* ARAT *sits on the chair and studies* HULET *coldly.* AMSET *retreats.* ARAT *is the Emperor.*)

HULET: Even though I was a high ceremonial official, behind my back they called me His Distinguished Majesty's cuckoo. That was because a Swiss clock, from which a cuckoo would jump out to announce each hour, hung in the Emperor's office. I had the honour to fulfil a similar duty during the hours that His Highness devoted to his Imperial duties. When the time came for the Emperor, in accordance with official protocol, to pass from one activity to another, I would come before him and bow several times. It was a signal to His Perspicacious Majesty that one hour was ending and that the time had come to start another.

(HULET *leaves.* FOST *makes another important entrance. He doesn't immediately see* ARAT *in the chair.*)

FOST: The Hour of the Ministers began at eleven o'clock and ended at noon. It was no trouble to call the ministers, since by custom these dignitaries stayed in the Palace all morning. Various ambassadors often complained of being unable to

visit a given minister in his office to take care of problems
because the secretary would invariably say, 'The Minister
has been summoned to the Emperor.' In point of fact, His
Gracious Highness liked to keep an eye on everyone, he liked
to keep everyone within reach. A minister who stayed away
from the Palace appeared in a bad light and never lasted long.
But the ministers, God knows, didn't try to stay away. No
one ever reached such a position without knowing the
monarch's likings and trying assiduously to comply with
them. Whoever wanted to climb the steps of the Palace had
first of all to master the negative knowledge: what was
forbidden to him and his subalterns, what was not to be said
or written, what should not be done, what should not be
overlooked or neglected. Only from such negative knowl-
edge could positive knowledge be born – but that positive
knowledge always remained obscure and worrisome, be-
cause no matter how well they knew what *not* to do, the
Emperor's favourites ventured only with extreme caution
and uncertainty into the area of propositions and postulates.
There they would immediately look to His Distinguished
Majesty, waiting to hear what he would say. And since His
Majesty had the habit of being silent, waiting, and post-
poning things, they too were silent, waited and postponed
things.

(FOST *watches the Emperor.* ARAT *doesn't move.* FOST *weakens,
moves away. The mood breaks.* AMSET *and* ARAT *and* FOST *are
students together.*)

AMSET: His Benevolent Highness would show favour to those
ministers who were not distinguished by quick wits or
perspicacity. He treated them as a stabilizing element in the
life of the Empire, while he himself, as everyone knows, was
always the champion of reform and progress. Reach, my
dear friend, for the autobiography dictated by the Emperor
in his last years and you will be convinced of

(UND *steps out for a moment. Returns with the volume.*)

how His Valiant Highness fought against the barbarity and
obscurantism that reigned in our country. Here is the Lon-
don edition of *My Life and Ethiopia's Progress*, translated by

Ullendorf. Here for example His Majesty mentions that at the beginning of his reign he forbade the customary punishment of cutting off hands and legs for even minor offences. Next, he writes that he forbade the custom that a man who had been accused of murder would have to be publicly executed by disembowelment, with the execution performed by the closest member of his family, so that, for example, a son would disembowel his father and a mother disembowel her son. To replace that custom, His Majesty instituted the office of state executioner, designated specific sites and procedures for executions, and stipulated that execution be only by shooting.

ARAT: Next, he purchased out of his own funds the first two printing presses and recommended that the first newspaper in the history of the country begin publication. Next, he opened the first bank. Next, he introduced electricity to Ethiopia, first in the palaces, and then in other buildings. Next, he abolished the custom of shackling prisoners in chains and iron stocks. From then on, prisoners were watched over by guards paid from the Imperial treasury. Next, he promulgated a decree condemning the slave trade. He decided to end that trade by 1950.

ARAT/UND/AMSET: 1950.

(*They pause looking at the air. One of them closes the book.* HULET *pops out from behind a tiny box window, looking eager.*)

HULET: And he kept on reforming: he abolished forced labour, he imported the first cars, he created a postal service.

(FOST *steps beside the box window.* HULET *looks nervously out.*)

FOST: Aah!

HULET: Ah!

FOST: Ah – unfortunately, driven by the desire for progress, His August Majesty committed a certain imprudence.

(HULET *is about to say something when* FOST *slams the little box door on him.*)

Because there used to be no state schools or universities in our country, the Emperor began sending young people abroad to study. These people would return home full of devious ideas, disloyal views, damaging plans, and unreasonable and disorderly projects. They would look at the Empire, put their heads in their hands and cry, 'Good God, how can anything like this exist?' Here you have, my friend, another proof of the ingratitude of youth. On the one hand so much care taken by His Majesty to give them access to knowledge, and on the other hand his reward in the form of shocking criticism, abusive sulking, undermining, and rejection. It's easy to imagine the bitterness with which these slanderers filled our monarch.

(*This time* HULET *makes an Imperial entrance.* FOST *bows. The others conduct the Emperor out.* AMSET *stays in the chair. All the doors close quietly around him.*)

AMSET: At one o'clock His Distinguished Highness left the Old Palace and proceeded to his residence, for dinner. The Emperor was accompanied by members of his family and dignitaries invited for the occasion. The Old Palace quickly emptied, silence filled the corridors, and the guards fell into their midday slumber.

(AMSET *settles in his chair and closes his eyes. The cuckoo clock strikes the hour. Lights up.*)

ACT TWO

After the Hour of Assignments, after the Hour of the Cashbox, after the Hour of the Supreme Court of Final Appeal, after the other hours, we have the Hour of the Purges.

A large cream sheet is draped over the bricked window. .There is a mundane photograph of the Emperor clumsily slapped against the wall. The chair is set downstage right. There is a Bible beneath it.

ARAT: 1960 was a woeful year, my friend. A venomous maggot began to infest the robust and succulent fruit of our Empire, and everything took such a morbid and irreparable course that instead of juice, alas, the fruit oozed blood.

(The upper part of the door where the cupboard stood is now a plain door. The blood commences to stream in a few long lines down the door. The blood doesn't quite reach to the floor. The blood stops. FOST stands alone. UND walks close by him. Glances at him.)

UND: Germane was one of those disloyal people who, upon returning to the Empire, threw up their hands in exasperation. But they did that secretly. In public they displayed loyalty, and in the Palace they said what was expected of them. And His August Majesty – oh, how I reproach him for it today – let himself be taken in. When Germane stood before him, His Compassionate Majesty looked on him with a loving eye and made him governor of a region in the southern province of Sidamo. The good soil there yields rich coffee. Hearing of this appointment, everyone in the Palace said that Our Omnipotent Ruler was laying open the path to the highest honours for the young man. Germane left with the Emperor's blessing, and at first things were quiet. After some time, though, dignitaries from the province of Sidamo began to appear. They came and loitered around the Palace, delicately dropping hints in conversational lulls – that Germane took bribes and used them to build schools. After all, it was understandable that a governor accepted tributes; all the dignitaries accepted tributes. But the abnormality of it was this, that a governor should use these tributes to build schools. Now, what if a second Germane springs up in a second province and starts to give away his bribes. Immediately we would have a mutiny of the dignitaries, protesting against this principle of giving away bribes. The result: the end of the Empire.

(AMSET *and* ARAT *have been listening.*)

AMSET/ARAT: Oh no.

(HULET *is the Emperor.* FOST *bows stiffly but with a sinister reserve.*)

AMSET: Germane was summoned to the capital for the Hour of Assignments and sent down to be governor of Jijiga, where he couldn't give away land because the only inhabitants were nomads. During the ceremony, Germane committed an offence that should have awakened the utmost vigilance in His August Majesty: after hearing his appointment read, Germane failed to kiss the monarch's hand.

ARAT: That evil spirit, together with his brother and a certain Captain Baye of the Imperial Guard, fled the City and remained in hiding for a week. They travelled only at night, for a price of five thousand dollars had

(FOST *walks backwards.* ARAT *wants to push him on further.* FOST *goes.*)

immediately been put on their heads and everyone was looking for them, since that is a great deal of money. They tried to make their way south, probably intending to cross into Kenya. But after a week, as they sat hidden in the bushes – not having eaten for several days and fainting from thirst, afraid to show themselves in any village to get food and water – they were captured by peasants who had been beating the bush to find them. When the peasants rushed forward to capture them, Germane shot Baye, then he shot his brother and finally he shot himself! His Majesty was informed of all this, and when he heard it he said that he wanted to see Germane's body. Accordingly, the corpse was brought to the Palace and thrown on the steps in front of the main entrance.

(UND *steps out to observe the unseen body on the steps.* AMSET *walks in step.*)

His Majesty came out and stood for a long time, looking at the body that was lying there. He remained silent, gazing without saying a word. Then the Emperor turned, as if he had been startled, and went back into the main building, ordering his lackeys to close the door. Later I saw Germane's body hanging from a tree in front of Saint George's Cathedral.

(UND *leaves.*)

HULET: That is when His Masterful Highness started a purge in the Palace. It was not an instantaneous and complete purge, because His Majesty opposed impious and noisy violence, preferring an exchange in careful doses, thought out, which would keep the old residents in check and in constant fear while at the same time opening the Palace to new people.

(HULET *remains there, frail, seemingly shrunken.*)

FOST: His Most Benevolent Highness no longer hurled people into dungeons, but very simply sent them home from the Palace, and this sending home meant condemnation to oblivion. Until that moment you were a man of the Palace, a prominent figure, a leader, someone important, influential, respected, talked about and listened to; all this gave one a feeling of existence, of presence in the world, of leading a full, important, useful life. Then His Highness summons you to the Hour of Assignments and sends you home for ever. Everything disappears in a second. You stop existing. Nobody will mention you, nobody will put you forward or show you any respect. You may say the same words you said yesterday, but though people listened to them devoutly, today they don't pay any attention. On the street, people pass you with indifference, and you can already see that the smallest provincial functionary can tell you to go to hell. His Majesty has changed you to a weak, defenceless

child and thrown you to a pack of jackals. Good luck!
(UND *enters. Sits.*)

UND: From the day Germane shot himself, a negative system
started operating between people and things. People seemed
unable to control things; things existed and ceased to exist in
their own malicious ways, slipping through people's hands.
Everyone felt helpless before the seemingly magic force by
which things autonomously appeared and disappeared, and
nobody knew how to master or break that force. This feeling
of helplessness, of always losing, always falling behind the
stronger, drives them deeper into negativism, into numb-
ness, into dejection, into depression, into hiding like par-
tridges. Even conversation deteriorated, losing its vigour
and momentum. Conversations started but somehow never
seemed to be completed. The Palace was sinking, and we all
felt it, we veterans in the service of His Venerable Majesty,
we whom fate had saved from the purge. We could feel the
temperature falling, life becoming more and more precisely
framed by ritual but more and more cut and dried, banal,
negative.

AMSET: Our Empire had existed for hundreds, even thousands,
of years without any noticeable development. However, the
world began to change. Everybody wanted to develop them-
selves. Our Emperor, infinitely infallible, noticed, and
generously agreed with this, seeing the advantages and
charms of costly novelty, and since he had always had a
weakness for all progress – indeed, he even liked progress –
his most honourably benevolent desire for action manifested
itself in the unconcealed desire to have a satiated and happy
people cry for years after, with full approval, 'Hey! Did he
ever develop us!'

ARAT: Thus, in the Hour of Development, between four and five
in the afternoon, His Highness showed particular vivacity
and keenness. He received processions of planners, econom-
ists and financial specialists, talking, asking questions, en-
couraging and praising. One was planning, another was
building, and so, in a word, development had started. And
how. His Indefatigable Majesty would ride out to open a

bridge here, a building there, an airport somewhere else, giving these structures his name:

HULET: The Haile Selassie Bridge in Ogaden.

FOST: The Haile Selassie Hospital in Harar.

UND: The Haile Selassie Hall in the capital.

ARAT: So that whatever was created bore his name. He also laid cornerstones, supervised construction, cut ribbons, took part in the ceremonial starting of a tractor.

(FOST *indicates the starting of a primitive tractor.* HULET *huffs and puffs and comes to a crashing halt, in the shape of a tractor.*

HULET *comes downstage.* FOST *and* AMSET *and* UND *and* ARAT *are behind him. They have become angry students and wild populace. They face the palace wall and move in slow dream steps.*)

HULET: Instead of showing their gratitude for the benefits of enlightenment, youngsters launched themselves on the turbid and treacherous waters of slander and faction. Alas, my friends, it is a sad truth that, despite His Majesty's having led the Empire on to the path of development, the students reproached the Palace for demagoguery and hypocrisy –

AMSET: How can one talk of development in the midst of utter poverty! What sort of development is it when the whole nation is being crushed by misery, whole provinces are starving, few can afford a pair of shoes, only a handful of subjects can read and write, anyone who falls seriously ill dies because there are neither hospitals nor physicians, ignorance and illiteracy hold sway everywhere, barbarity, humiliation, trampling underfoot, despotism, exploitation, desperation.

HULET: And on and on in this tone. Reproaching, calumniating ever more arrogantly, they spoke out against sweetening and dressing things up – taking advantage of His Clement Highness, who only rarely ordered that the mutinous rabble which spilled from the university gates in a larger mass each year be fired upon. The time came when they brought out their impudent whim of reforming. Development, they said, is impossible without reform.

(*The rioters slowly grasp stones and objects and hurl them at the Palace wall in a slow dream state.*)

AMSET: Give the peasants land!

UND: Abolish privileges!

FOST: Democratize society!

ARAT: Liquidate feudalism!

(FOST *and* ARAT *haul* AMSET *off as if he has been too brave.* AMSET *snatches the photograph of the Emperor from off the wall. They drag* AMSET *clear.* UND *steps towards us murmuring intently.*)

UND: And as a consequence of Our Benefactor's concern to develop the forces of order and thanks to his great generosity in that area, the number of policemen multiplied during the last years of his reign, and ears appeared everywhere, sticking up out of the ground, glued to the walls, flying through the air, hanging on doorknobs, hiding in offices, lurking in crowds, standing in doorways

(*Two feet emerge through the gap between the floor and a door. He stops. The feet slowly move away.*)

jostling in the market place. To protect themselves from the plague of informers, people learned – without anyone knowing how or where, or when, without schools, without courses, without records or dictionaries – another language, mastered it, and became so fluent in it that we simple and uneducated folk suddenly became a bilingual nation. It was extremely helpful; it even saved lives and preserved peace and allowed people to exist. Each of the two languages had a different vocabulary, a different set of meanings, even a different grammar, and yet everyone overcame these difficulties and learned to express himself in the proper language. One tongue served for external speech, the other for internal. The first was sweet and the second bitter, the first polished and the second coarse, one allowed to come to the surface and the other kept out of sight.

(*Even more intensely,* ARAT *hastens forward.* UND *slinks away as if not daring to glance back at* ARAT.)

ARAT: Reports are coming in from Gojam Province that the peasants are brawling, rebelling, bashing in the skulls of tax collectors, hanging policemen, running dignitaries out of town, burning down estates, uprooting crops. The governor reports that rebels are storming the offices and that whenever they get their hands on the Emperor's people, they vilify them, torture them, and quarter them. Obviously, the longer the submissiveness, the silence and the shouldering of burdens, the greater the hostility and cruelty. And in the capital the students defend the rebels, praising them, pointing a finger at the court, hurling insults. Fortunately, that province is so situated that it can be cut off, surrounded by the army, shot up, and bled into submission. But until that was accomplished you could sense a great fear in the Palace, because you can never tell how far boiling water will spill.

(HULET *slips out from the side. Acquires diplomatic outrage.*)

HULET: In the summer of 1973 a certain Jonathan 'Dimblyby', a journalist from London television, came to our country. He had visited the Empire before and made commendable films about His Supreme Majesty, and so it occurred to no one that such a journalist, who had earlier praised, would dare to criticize later. But such is obviously the dastardly nature of people without dignity or faith. Anyway, this time, instead of showing how His Highness attends to development and cares for the prosperity of the little ones, 'Dimblyby' went up north, from where he supposedly returned perturbed and shaken. Right away he left for England. A month hadn't passed when a report came from our Embassy there that Mr 'Dimblyby' had shown a film entitled *Ethiopia: The Unknown Famine* on London TV, in which this unprincipled calumniator pulled the demagogic trick of showing thousands of people dying of hunger, and next to that His Venerable Highness feasting with dignitaries. Then he showed roads on which scores of poor, famished skeletons were lying, and immediately afterwards our airplanes bringing champagne and caviare from Europe. Here you can see, my friend, the irresponsibility of the foreign press, which like Mr 'Dimblyby' praised our monarch for years and then suddenly, without any rhyme or reason, condemned him. Why? Why such treason and immorality? The Embassy reports that a whole planeload of European 'Dimblybies' is taking off from London, to come and see death from hunger, to know our reality, and to determine where the money goes that their government has given to His August Majesty for development, catching up, and surpassing. Bluntly speaking, interference in the internal affairs of the Empire! In the Palace, commotion and indignation, but His Most Singular Highness counsels calm and discretion. Now we await the highest decisions. Right away voices sound for recalling the ambassador, who sent such unpleasant and alarming reports and brought so much unrest into the Palace.

(AMSET *and* FOST *and* ARAT *and* UND *become dignitaries. They collect in diplomatic corners behind* HULET.)

However, the Minister of Foreign Affairs argues that such a recall will put fear into the remaining ambassadors and make them all stop reporting, and yet His Venerable Highness needs to know what is said about him in various parts of the world. Next the members of the Crown Council speak up, demanding that the airplane carrying the journalists be turned back and that none of the blasphemous rabble be let into the Empire.

UND: How can we not let them in? They'll raise hell and condemn His Gracious Majesty more than ever.

FOST: Let them in, but deny them the hunger.

SOME: No.

OTHERS: Yes.

FOST: Keep them in Addis Ababa, show them the development and let them write only what can be read in our newspapers. We have a loyal press, yes?

ALL: Yes.

(FOST *steps towards us.*)

FOST: To tell the truth, there wasn't much of it. Because for over thirty million subjects twenty-five thousand copies were printed daily, but His Highness worked on the assumption that even the most loyal press should not be given in abundance, because that might create a habit of reading, and from there it is only a single step to the habit of thinking.

ALL: Correct.

(ARAT *steps forward.*)

ARAT: A press conference took place.

AMSET: (*Acquires a Western voice*) What does the problem of death from hunger which decimates the population look like?

UND: (*Becomes a minister*) I know nothing of any such matter!

ARAT: (*To us*) Answers the Minister of Information, and I must tell you my friends that he wasn't far from the truth.

(AMSET *becomes a minister and the others crowd behind him giving him advice.* AMSET *finds he is placating a crowd of people and he is at his most reassuring.*)

AMSET: First of all death from hunger has existed in our Empire for hundreds of years, an everyday, natural thing, and it never occurs to anyone to make any noise about it. Drought comes. And the earth dries up. The cattle die. The peasants starve. Ordinary, in accordance with the laws of nature and the eternal order of things. Since this is eternal and normal none of the dignitaries would dare to bother His Most Exalted Highness with the news that in such and such a province a given person had died of hunger.

(UND *sees a member of the crowd who seeks an answer to a question. He points the person out to* AMSET.)

Of course, His Benevolent Highness visited the provinces himself, but it was not his custom to stop in poor regions where there was hunger. And anyway, how much can one see during an official visit?

(ARAT *breaks clear and speaks to us and* AMSET.)

ARAT: 'Can we,' ask the correspondents, 'go north?'

AMSET: (*Angry*) No you can't – eh! –

UND: The roads are full of – eh! –

FOST: (*Grasping for a straw*) Bandits!

(*They congratulate each other.*)

ARAT: He wasn't far from the truth. Because increased incidents of armed disloyalty near highways all over the Empire had been much reported of late. And then the ministers took them for an excursion around the capital, showing them factories and praising development. But with that gang, forget it! They don't want development. They demand hunger and that's all there is to it.

(HULET *scuttles around the stage showing the correspondents the town. The correspondents circle around* HULET. *He despairs.*)

HULET: Well, you won't get hunger! How can there be hunger if there is development?

ARAT: So a scandal broke out. We could no longer say that there is no hunger. And once more the correspondents attack. They wave their photographs in the air –

(AMSET *and* FOST *and* UND *become the enraged correspondents. They surround* HULET.)

AMSET: What has the government done about hunger!

HULET: His Most Supreme Majesty has attached the utmost importance to the matter.

FOST/UND/AMSET: But specifically what!

HULET: His Majesty will announce in due time his intended Royal decisions, assignments and directions, because it is not fitting for ministers to do so.

AMSET: (*To us*) The correspondents flew away, without seeing

(FOST *and* UND *depart indignantly.*)

hunger close up. And this whole affair, conducted so smoothly and in such a dignified manner, the Minister considered a success and our press called a victory, which was fine, but we feared that if the Minister were to disappear tomorrow we would have nothing but sorrow. And that was exactly what happened later, when the rebels put him up against the wall.

ARAT: Great discontent, even condemnation and indignation, reigned in the Palace because of the disloyalty of European governments, which allowed Mr Dimbleby and his ilk to raise a din on the subject of starvation. His Most Sovereign Highness attached the greatest importance to hunger. So we eagerly entered on the new road and asked the foreign benefactors for help. Not much time had passed before good news came. Airplanes loaded with wheat landed, ships full of flour and sugar sailed in. Physicians and missionaries came, people from philanthropic organizations, students from foreign colleges, and also foreign correspondents disguised as male nurses. The whole crowd marched north to the provinces of Tigre and Welo, and also east to Ogaden, where, they say, whole tribes had perished of hunger.

HULET: The trivial event that set things off was a fashion show at the university, organized by the American Peace Corps even though all meetings and gatherings were forbidden. But His Distinguished Majesty could not forbid the Americans a show, could he? And so the students took advantage of this cheerful and carefree event to gather in an enormous crowd and set off for the Palace. And from that moment on they never again let themselves be driven back to their homes. They held meetings, they stormed implacably and vehemently, they did not yield again. For them there existed only the twentieth century, or perhaps even this twenty-first century everyone is waiting for in which blessed justice will reign. Nothing else suited them any more, everything else irritated them. They didn't see what they wanted to see, and so, apparently, they decided to arrange the world so that they would be able to look at it with contentment. Oh well, young people, very young people.

FOST: The last year! Yes, but who then could have foreseen that 1974 would be our last year? Well, yes, one did feel a sort of vagueness, a melancholy chaotic ineptness, a certain negativity, something heavy in the air, nervousness and tension, flabbiness, now dawning, now growing dark, but how did we go so quickly straight into the abyss? In January 1974 General Beleta Abebe stopped over in the Gode barracks on his way to an inspection in Ogaden. The next day an incredible report came to the Palace: the general has been arrested by the soldiers, who are forcing him to eat what they eat. Food so obviously rotten that some fear the general will fall ill and die.

UND: On top of all this, like a bolt from the blue, comes the news that the Second Division has rebelled in Eritrea. They occupy Asmara, arrest their general, lock up the provincial governor, and make a godless proclamation over the radio. They demand justice, pay rises and humane funerals. The problem of burial had existed for a long time, which is to say that in order to limit excessive war expenses, only officers had a right to a funeral, while the bodies of the common soldiers were left to the vultures and the hyenas. Such inequality now caused a rebellion. The following day the navy joins the rebels and the avalanche rolls on, my dear sir, because that very day the air force mutinies. Airplanes buzz the city and, according to rumour, drop bombs. The next day, our biggest and most important division, the Fourth, rebels and immediately surrounds the capital, demanding a raise and insisting that the ministers and other dignitaries be brought to court because, the soldiers say, they corrupted themselves in an ugly way and should stand in the pillory of public opinion.

(AMSET *pushes nervously forward from behind a door, afraid lest he is already overheard. Somewhere behind him a small box opens and an ear leans intently forward trying to catch his words.*)

AMSET: Three factions appear in the Palace. The first, the Jailers, are a fierce and inflexible coterie who demand the restoration of order and insist on arresting the malcontents, putting them behind bars, beating and hanging them. A second faction coalesces, the Talkers, a coterie of liberals: weak people and philosophizers, who think that one should invite the rebels to sit down at a table and talk, listen to what they say, and improve the Empire. Finally, the third faction is made up of Floaters, who, I would say, are the most numerous group in the Palace. They don't think at all, but hope that like corks in the water they will float on the waves of circumstance.

(AMSET *does not appear to have noticed he has been overheard. The box door where the ear is closes softly.*)

ARAT: In those days His Majesty rose from his bed with ever-increasing difficulty. Night after night he slept badly or not at all, and then he would nod off during the day. He said nothing to us, not even during meals, which he ate surrounded by his family. And so, my friend, in the middle of these suddenly unleashed intrigues that plunged the whole court into bitter fighting, no one thought about what was going on in the Empire. Quite unexpectedly and surprisingly the army enters the town at night and arrests all ministers of the old government. They even lock up two hundred generals and high-ranking officers – distinguished in their unfaltering loyalty to the Emperor. Nobody has had time to recover from the blow when news comes that the conspirators have arrested the Chief of the General Staff. In the Palace – an atmosphere of terror, fear, confusion, depression. The Jailers are pressing the Emperor to do something, to order the rescue of those who have been imprisoned, to drive away the students, and to hang the conspirators. His Benevolent Majesty hears out all the advice, nods his assent, gives comfort. The Talkers say that it's the last chance to sit down at the table, bring the conspirators around to one's own point of view, and repair and improve the Empire. These too, His Benevolent Majesty hears out, nodding approval, comforting. Days go by and the conspirators lead first one person then another out of the Palace and arrest them.

(HULET *makes his way towards us. More serious now. Behind him* FOST *and* AMSET *and* UND *and* ARAT *assume ministerial postures.*)

HULET: Suddenly His Majesty summons his counsellors, reprimands them for neglecting development, and after giving them a scolding, announces that we are going to construct dams on the Nile. But how can we erect dams, the confused advisers grumble, when the provinces are starving, the nation is restless, the Talkers are whispering about straightening out the Empire, and the officers are conspiring and rounding up the notables? Immediately, audacious rumours are heard in the corridors saying that it would be better to help the starving and forget about the dams. To this the Finance Minister replies that if the dams are built it will be possible to let water into the fields and such an abundant harvest will result that there will be no more death from starvation.

FOST: Well, yes, but how long will it take to build the dams? In the meantime the nation will die of hunger.

AMSET: The nation isn't going to die. It hasn't died yet, so it isn't going to die now. And if we don't build the dams, how are we going to catch up and surpass?

UND: But against whom are we supposed to be racing anyway?

AMSET: What do you mean, 'whom'? Egypt, of course!

UND: But Egypt, sir, is wealthier than we are! And even Egypt couldn't put up dams out of its own pocket! Where are we supposed to find the funds for our dams!

(AMSET *becomes the senior minister here and produces a silent tirade*.)

HULET: Here the Minister really lost his temper with the doubting, and began lecturing them, telling them how important it is to sacrifice oneself for development.

AMSET: Besides, His Majesty has ordered, has he not, that we all develop constantly, without resting even for a moment, putting our hearts and souls into it.

HULET: And the Minister of Information immediately announced His Venerable Majesty's decision as a new success, and I remember that in the twinkling of an eye the following slogan appeared in the streets of the capital:

(FOST *and* AMSET *and* UND *and* ARAT *march downstage and address us in a loud ringing chorus*.)

ALL: As soon as the work on the dam is done,
Wealth will accrue to everyone!
Let the slanderers spew their lies and shams,
They will suffer in hell for opposing our dams!

(*They growl at us and leave.* FOST *turns back*.)

FOST: The whole world stood on its head, strange signs appeared in the sky. The moon and Jupiter, stopping in the seventh and twelfth houses instead of turning in the direction of the triangle, began ominously to form the figure of a square. Accordingly, the Indians who explained the signs at court now fled the Palace, probably because they were afraid to disturb His Venerable Majesty with a bad omen. The dignitaries ran through the Palace perturbed, upsetting His August Majesty, urging him to order imprisonments and hangings. And the remaining Jailers also pressed His Noble Majesty – and even begged him on their knees – to stop the conspirators, to put them behind bars. They were completely dumbfounded, however, completely unable to understand, when they saw that His Most Singular Majesty wore his military uniform all the time (medals jingling) and carried his marshal's baton, as if he wanted to show that he still commanded his army, still stood at its head, and still gave the orders. His Venerable Majesty wanted to rule over everything. Even if there was a rebellion, he wanted to rule over the rebellion, to command a mutiny, even if it was directed against his own reign.

(FOST *pauses. Turns away.* UND *tiptoes forward. He whispers, afraid to raise his voice.*)

UND: The salons, corridors and galleries grew more deserted each day, and yet nobody took up the defence of the Palace. Nobody gave the call to close the doors and break out the weapons. People looked at one another thinking, 'Perhaps they'll take him and leave me alone. And if I raise a hue and cry against the rebels, they'll lock me up right away and leave the others in peace. So it's better to keep quiet and not know anything. Better not to leap, in order not to weep. Better to keep your peace, and avoid an early decease.'

(*The stage is empty.* AMSET *emerges. As he speaks,* HULET *is led forth as the Emperor. He wears an Imperial topee, not necessarily an exact fit, and a scarlet ribbon with a medal.* FOST *and* UND *and* ARAT *escort him.* FOST *holds up the cream parasol.* HULET *moves his lips. A barely audible murmur of words and consolations comes from his mouth.*)

AMSET: It was raining that day, a chilly rain, and mist floated in the air as His Majesty stepped out on to the balcony to make his speech. Next to him stood only a handful of soaked, depressed dignitaries – the rest were in prison or had fled the capital. There was no crowd, only the Palace servants and some soldiers from the Imperial Guard standing at the edge of an empty courtyard. His August Majesty expressed his compassion for the starving provinces and said that he would not neglect any chance to keep the Empire developing fruitfully. He also thanked the army for its loyalty, praised his subjects, encouraged them and wished them good luck. But he spoke so quietly that through the steady rain one could hardly make out individual words. And know, my friend, that I will take this memory to the grave with me, because I can still hear how His Majesty's voice breaks, and I can see how tears stream down his venerable face. And then, yes, then, for the first time, I thought to myself that everything was really coming to an end. That on this rainy day all life is seeping away, we are covered with cold, clinging fog, and the moon and Jupiter have stopped in the seventh and twelfth houses to form a square.

(HULET *hands his topee and sash to* UND. ARAT *breaks away. Downstage.*)

ARAT: Amid all the depression, with the sense of being crushed and pushed against a wall, there suddenly arrived the Swedish physicians whom His Most Exceptional Majesty had summoned long ago to lead calisthenics at court. But it was the desire of His Majesty and the Crown Council, just then, that all the Palace people should take very good care of their health, take full advantage of the blessings of nature, rest as much as necessary in comfort and affluence, breathe good – and preferably foreign – air.

(FOST *and* UND *and* AMSET *have taken off their jackets. They enter behind* ARAT *and lie down on the floor. They put their legs in the air. Point their bums at us. And wiggle their toes. They also wriggle their wrists and fingers. Slowly they sway from side to side in a rhythmic portrayal of dead ants in a last ritual of gymnastic pain.*)

We, the last handful of people remaining in the Palace, had to fall in for morning calisthenics and force the greatest treasure of the Empire into supple fitness by moving our arms and legs about.

(HULET *looks quite undignified. He also tries to rock his legs back and forth in a vain attempt to join the others. The others are exhausted.*)

HULET: But the worst thing about the calisthenics was that when a group of courtiers gathered in a salon to wave their arms and legs about, the conspirators would march in and drive everyone off to jail. To prevent the rebels from capturing everyone at once, the Grand Chamberlain of the court pulled off a cunning trick by ordering that calisthenics be done in small groups. So if some fell into the trap, others would be saved.

(*The heroes of the calisthenics retreat aching.* FOST *comes downstage gripping his pains.*)

FOST: And so came the month of August, the last weeks of power for our supreme ruler. But do I really express myself well, using the word 'power' about those last days of decline? It's so very difficult to establish where the borderline runs between true power that subdues everything, power that creates the world or destroys it – where the borderline is between living power, great, even terrifying, and the appearance of power, the empty pantomime of ruling, being one's own dummy, only playing the role, not seeing the world, not hearing it, merely looking into oneself. And it is still more difficult to say when omnipotence becomes powerlessness, good fortune – adversity, lustre – tarnish. That is exactly what no one in the Palace could sense, since all gazes were so fixed that in powerlessness they saw omnipotence, in adversity – good fortune, in tarnish – lustre. And even if someone had a different perception, how could he, without risking his head, fall to the ground

(FOST *sweats and kneels down. The panic grips him.*)

at our monarch's feet and say, 'Your Majesty, you are already powerless, surrounded by adversity, becoming tarnished!'? The problem in the Palace was that we had no access to the truth.

(*He creeps away. The stage empties. Change of mood. One by one they come back.* UND *trails a long cream sheet behind him across the floor.* HULET *and* ARAT *and* AMSET *follow.* HULET *trails a sheet. So does* AMSET. ARAT *takes the long sheet down from across the bricked window.* UND *comes downstage. As he does so the others drape their sheets around each other and recline in the gloom like ancient furnishings wrapped up for a long absence.*)

UND: The Palace had become the last refuge for dignitaries and notables from the whole Empire, who came here hoping to be safer at His Majesty's side, hoping that the Emperor would save them and obtain their freedom through his entreaties to the arrogant officers. Without respect for their honours and titles, dignitaries and favourites of all ranks, levels and distinctions now slept side by side on the carpets, sofas and armchairs, covering themselves with curtains and drapes – over which they got into constant quarrels, since some didn't want the curtains taken down from the windows for fear the rebellious air force would bomb the Palace if it were not kept blacked out. The others maintained that they couldn't fall asleep without covers, and they selfishly pulled down the curtains and covered themselves. All these squabbles and gibes were meaningless, however, because the officers soon reconciled everyone by taking them to jail, where the contentious dignitaries couldn't count on any covers.

(UND *draws the sheet over himself. He finds a wall to lean against. He sinks there.*)

I lived through the blackest days of that last month as an official in the Ministry of Palace Provisions. And let me tell you that it was impossible to ascertain the number of people in our court, since the roster of dignitaries changed every day – some sneaked into the Palace counting on help, others were taken off to jail, and often someone who had sneaked in overnight would be in jail by noon.

(HULET *makes his way between the inert sheeted figures. He is lost and quite without direction. He looks around him.*)

HULET: Life inside the Palace seemed strange, as if existing only of itself and for itself. When I went into town as an official of the Palace post office, I would see normal life – cars driving through the streets, children playing, people selling and buying, old men sitting, talking away – and every day I would pass from one existence to another, no longer knowing which one was real, and feeling that it was sufficient for me to go into the city, to mingle with the crowds, for the whole Palace to vanish from memory. It would disappear, as if it didn't exist, to the point of making me anxious that when I came back I wouldn't find it there.

(AMSET *and* FOST *and* HULET *and* UND *take their shawls and fade away through the doors like cowled secrets.* ARAT *takes off his shawl.*)

ARAT: He spent the last days alone in the Palace, with only his old *valet de chambre* for company. Apparently the group in favour of closing the Palace and dethroning the Emperor had gained the upper hand in the Dergue. None of the names of the officers was known, none was announced – they acted in

77

total secrecy until the end. Now they say that this group was headed by a young major named Mengistu Haile-Mariam. There were

(*Behind* ARAT *steps along* UND *as Mengistu. He stands before* HULET, *who becomes the Emperor.* UND *has a small army baton.*) other officers, too, but they are all dead. I remember when this Mariam would come to the Palace as a captain. His mother was a servant at the court. I cannot tell who made it possible for him to graduate from the officers' school. Slender, slight, always tense, but in control of himself – anyway, that was the impression he gave. He knew the structure of the court, he knew who was who, he knew whom to arrest and when in order to prevent the Palace from functioning, to make it lose its power and strength, change it into a useless simulacrum that today stands abandoned and deteriorating.

(ARAT *lays his cream shawl down on the stage as flat as possible. He stands back against the wall.* HULET *comes towards us.* UND *and* AMSET *and* FOST *become military officers and scrutinize the audience.*)

HULET: The crucial decisions of the Military Committee must have been taken some time around the first of August. The Military Committee – that is, the Dergue – was composed of a hundred and twenty delegates elected at meetings in divisions and garrisons. They had a list of five hundred dignitaries and courtiers whom they gradually arrested, creating a sinking emptiness around the Emperor until finally he was left alone in the Palace.

(*Lights change. A harsh bright interrogative light shreds the floor.* HULET *becomes the Emperor.* UND *becomes the loyal old man-servant.* FOST *and* AMSET *and* ARAT *are the soldiers inside the Palace now.*)

FOST: In those days, only the officers intruded. First they would come to me, asking to be announced to His Unparalleled Majesty, and then they would enter the office, where His Highness would seat them in comfortable armchairs. Then they would read a proclamation demanding that His Benevolent Majesty give back the money that, they claim, he has been illegally appropriating for fifty years, depositing in banks around the world and concealing in the Palace and in the homes of dignitaries and notables. This, they say, should be returned because it is the property of the people, from whose blood and sweat it came. 'What money are you talking about?' His Benevolent Majesty asks. 'Everything went for development, for catching up and surpassing, and the development was proclaimed a success, was it not? We had no money for ourselves.' 'Some development!' cry the officers. And they get up from the armchairs, lift the great Persian carpet –

(AMSET *and* ARAT *roll back the cream sheet on the floor, fold the sheet and hold it up. They look down at* HULET *who grimaces as if he has never seen all this money before.*)

AMSET/FOST/ARAT: Tsk . . . tsk . . . tsk.

FOST: – from the floor, and there under the carpet are rolls of dollar bills stuck together, one next to the other, so that the floor looks green. In the presence of His August Majesty, they order the sergeants to count the money, write down the amount, and carry it off to be nationalized.

(FOST *and* AMSET *and* ARAT *march away.*)

UND: They leave soon afterwards, and His Dignified Majesty calls me into his office and orders me to hide among his books the money he used to keep in his desk. Since His Majesty, as the designated descendant of Solomon, had a great collection of the Holy Scriptures, translated into many languages, that's where we stashed away the money. Ah, those officers, clever

(UND *is still the old loyal servant.* FOST *and* ARAT *and* AMSET *march back in.*)

sharks they were! The following day they come, read their proclamation, and demand the return of the money, because, they say, it's needed to buy flour for the starving. His Majesty, sitting at his desk, shows them the empty drawers. At which the officers spring from their chairs, grab all those Bibles from the bookcases, and shake the dollars out, whereupon the sergeants count them, write down the figures, and take them away to be nationalized.

(FOST *pushes* UND *away and empties books on the floor and dollars fall everywhere.* FOST *talks to us. Then he talks back to* HULET *who is still the Emperor.*)

FOST: All this is nothing, say the officers. The rest of the money should be returned, especially the amounts in the Swiss and British banks in His Majesty's private account, estimated at half a billion dollars. They persuade His Majesty to sign the appropriate cheques, and thus,

(AMSET *and* ARAT *mime chequebooks and pens.* HULET *mimes he has never seen a chequebook or a pen in his life.*)

they claim, the money will be returned to the nation. 'Where am I to come up with all this money?' asks His Venerable Majesty. 'All I have is a few pennies for the care of my ailing son in a Swiss hospital.' 'Pretty pennies they are too,' answer the officers, and they read aloud a letter from the Swiss Embassy which says that His Majesty has on account in banks there the sum of one hundred million dollars. So they go on quarrelling until finally His Majesty falls into meditation, closes his eyes, and stops breathing. Then the officers withdraw, promising to return.

(FOST *and* AMSET *and* ARAT *leave.* HULET *closes his eyes. Opens one weary eye and beadily looks out at us.* UND, *the old servant, searches the bricked-up window. Looks down at the crowds below. The stage darkens.*)

UND: Silence fell on the Palace, but a bad silence in which one could hear the shouts from the street. Demonstrators were marching through the town, all sorts of rabble loitering about cursing His Majesty, calling him a thief, wanting to string him up from a tree. 'Crook! Give us back our money!' they cried. 'Hang the Emperor! Hang the Emperor!' Then I would close all the windows in the Palace to prevent these indecent and slanderous cries from reaching His Venerable Majesty's ears, from stirring his blood. And I would quickly lead my lord to the chapel, which was in the most secluded place, and to muffle the blasphemous roar, I would read aloud to him the words of the prophets.

(UND *slowly guides* HULET *towards a lighter corner of the stage.*

There is a Bible set beneath the chair. They crouch there. UND *finds the page.* UND *reads first. He is always about two complete sentences in front of* HULET. *They recite together.*)

UND/HULET: 'Also take no heed unto all words that are spoken, lest thou hear thy servant curse thee. They are vanity and the work of errors; in the time of their visitation they shall perish. Remember, O Lord, what is come upon us: consider, and behold our reproach. The joy of our heart is ceased: our dance is turned into mourning. The crown is fallen from our head: for this our heart is faint; for these things our eyes are dim. How is the gold become dim! How is the most fine gold changed! The stones of the sanctuary are poured out in the top of every street. They that were brought up in scarlet embrace dunghills. Thou hast seen all their vengeance and all their imaginations against me. Thou hast heard their reproach, O Lord; the lips of those that rose up against me; I am their musick. They have cut off my life in the dungeon, and cast a stone upon me.

HULET: (*Some sentences behind still, as* UND *stops*) '. . . Thou hast heard their reproach, O Lord; the lips of those that rose up against me; I am their musick. They have cut off my life in the dungeon, and cast a stone upon me.'

UND: And as His August Majesty listened, he would doze off. There I would leave him, proceeding to my lodgings to hear what was being said on the radio. In those days the radio was the only link between the Palace and the Empire.

(*Light changes.* FOST *enters as a soldier.* ARAT *too.* AMSET. *Light is harsh now.* HULET *cowers by the chair, half seated.* UND *tries to protect him.*)

FOST: At the end of August the military proclaimed the nationalization of all the Emperor's palaces. There were fifteen of them. His private enterprises met the same fate. Among them –

UND: The St George Brewery.

ARAT: The Addis Ababa Metropolitan Bus Company.

(HULET *lifts up his face from its strange slumber.*)

HULET: (*Softly, but with a certain regret*) The Mineral Water Factory in Ambo.

(AMSET *forward.* UND *turns the chair around so that* HULET *can be positioned properly.*)

AMSET: The officers came to the Palace and announced that in the evening the television would show a film that the Emperor should watch. His Imperial Highness willingly agreed to fulfil the request. He sat down in his armchair to watch the programme. It was *Ethiopia: The Unknown Famine* by Jonathan Dimbleby.

(UND *switches on the TV set in the air. The others watch.* ARAT *murmurs a gentle barely audible incantation of the TV programme as if heard from a distance: the music, the soundtrack, the voice of the commentator.* HULET *hears the last murmurs from* ARAT. *There is a clearly heard 'goodnight' in the murmur.* UND *turns off the TV set.*)

HULET: Goodnight.

(AMSET *becomes an officer.*)

AMSET: At daybreak three officers in combat uniforms made their way to the chamber where the Emperor had been since dawn. After a preliminary bow, one of them read out the Act of Dethronement. The Emperor heard out the officer's words, and then he expressed his thanks to everyone, and added that if the revolution was good for the people then he, too, supported the revolution and would not oppose the dethronement. 'In that case,' said the officer, 'His Imperial Majesty will please follow us.'

(HULET *becomes the Emperor. The officers study him with a mixture of awe and contempt.*)

In the driveway stood a green Volkswagen. An officer opened the door and held the front seat, so that the Emperor could get in the back.

(FOST *as an officer opens the car door and pulls back the front seat.*)

HULET: I'm supposed to go like this?

(HULET *slowly moves.*)

ARAT: The Volkswagen set off, preceded by a jeep full of armed soldiers, towards the Fourth Division Barracks.

(HULET *is led away slowly by* UND *the old retainer.*)

FOST: It wasn't seven o'clock yet. They were driving through empty streets. With a gesture of his hand, His Imperial

Highness greeted those few people they passed along the way.

(HULET *and* UND *leave.* UND *returns, quickly putting on dark glasses.* AMSET *and* FOST *and* ARAT *stand side by side. They are military.*)

UND: (*As a soldier*) Everybody left the Palace.

(*They face us. Turn away. Slowly exit through one door each. Bright light floods through from each door left open. The chair casts its shadow across the stage. The light is bleak and cold.*)

END

ADDITIONAL SCENE

This scene has not yet been included in the text. It may perhaps be placed in Act Two.

AMSET, *who indicated the figure of Makonen in Act One, is placed on the floor. Only his head appears above the floor line of the stage.*

AMSET: I am Makonen. A strange personage. Now deceased. A minister. One of the select few. I dedicated all my time to fostering my private network of informers. In offices, in the army, in the police force. Sleeping little, wearing myself out, until I looked like a shadow. I penetrated quietly. Like a mole. Without theatricality, without rodomontade, grey, sour, hidden in the dusk. Myself like the dusk. I had as much claim to the royal ear as I wanted. Yes . . .
  (*He turns to the side. Dips his chin to the ground. We see a trickle of blood from his ear.* HULET *and* UND *and* ARAT *and* FOST *study the head on the ground. The light is strange. They seem to tremble together.*)

FOR THE WEST (UGANDA)

'Now I have had this dream . . . I know the day I am going to die, and who does this to me. Prophet John has told me, also. That is why it must be top secret I'm afraid . . .'

Field Marshal Doctor Idi Amin 'Dada'
President for Life of Uganda
23 August 1973

CHARACTERS

FIELD MARSHAL DOCTOR AL-HAJJI IDI
AMIN 'DADA', DSO, MC, VC, CBE,
COMMANDER-IN-CHIEF OF THE
ARMED FORCES, MINISTER OF
DEFENCE, AND PRESIDENT FOR LIFE
OF UGANDA

MAJOR GEORGE 'AMOS' TODD
GREVILLE WILLIAM ALLNUTT
ISAID DEM ALA-MESSID JALLI
VOICE OF THE PRESIDENT'S
SECRETARY

★

The characters who appear in the dream se-
quence, and who belong to the President's im-
agination, are called ANGUS FRASER and SINDI
BARU.

For the West (Uganda) was first presented at the Theatre Upstairs, London, on 18 May 1977; and at the Cottesloe stage, National Theatre, on 13 August 1977, with the following cast:

FIELD MARSHAL DOCTOR IDI AMIN 'DADA', PRESIDENT FOR LIFE OF UGANDA	Rudolph Walker
MAJOR GEORGE 'AMOS' TODD	Basil Henson
GREVILLE WILLIAM ALLNUTT	Roger Milner
ISAID DEM ALA-MESSID JALLI	Renu Setna
VOICE OF THE PRESIDENT'S SECRETARY	Fumi Layo

DIRECTOR	Nicholas Wright
DESIGNER	Anne-Marie Schöne

ACT ONE
Idi's Dream

IDI *is asleep in medalled splendour. A long balcony view. Nothing obstructs the view. It is beautiful. There are British cartoons framed against the walls. A large desk. An intercom. Various white plastic soft chairs. Intercom on.*

VOICE: (*Indicate dream*) Yes, Mr President.

IDI: (*Indicate dream*) What you got out there?

VOICE: The British Delegation, Mr President. A Forward Delegation come prepare for next month talks on compensation.

IDI: What their names?

VOICE: Major George Amos Todd. Dr Angus Fraser. Mr Sindi Baru. You will find all the necessary papers on your desk.

IDI: You send them in right away.

VOICE: At once, Mr President.

> (*Fade for the dream sequence. Lights again.* AMOS *and* ANGUS *and* SINDI *carry* IDI *on stage. They carry him seated on a giant board. They lower* IDI*. The* MAJOR *is in uniform.* FRASER *in white shirt Commonwealth Office diplomacy bespoke.* IDI *effusive.*)

AMOS: (*Indicate dream*) Sir!

IDI: My old Commander friend!

AMOS: That's right, sir!

IDI: The Major Amos who taught us all how to put the famous Sandhurst British boot in.

AMOS: King's African Rifles, sir, out in Karamoja. And how we smashed the Suk and the Askari, sir!

IDI: B Company No. 4 King's Africans. And that night I was sergeant we took those members the Central Legislative

Assembly out fact-finding they call it, and in the night a lion
creep in and eat all their underwear.

AMOS: I right recall how you polished him off, that lion, sir.
From the top of the Land Rover –

IDI: Only damn safe place to be.

AMOS: Fair good to best aim that was, sir.

IDI: Big ·375 rifle. Up the throaty. Those bullets could throw a
man . . . Who we got here?

AMOS: Dr Angus Fraser from the Commonwealth Office. East
Africa speciality. Eight years' service in Nairobi.

IDI: What rank you have in the British Commonwealth Office?

ANGUS: (*Indicate dream*) Sir, Mr President . . . First Secretary
(East African Advisory Board) and direct liaison with the
Assistant Under-Secretary of State, Foreign and Common-
wealth Office. The Under-Secretary and I are –

IDI: Very pleased to have you here. Hope you didn't have long to
wait. Some peoples think it not safe to come here see Amin.

ANGUS: It is an honour to visit your beautiful country, Mr
President. What Winston Churchill called 'the pearl of
Africa'.

AMOS: And . . . Mr Sindi Baru. Delegate to the United Nations
High Commission for Refugees. Representative of the
Disenfranchised Asian Communities –

IDI: Dis –

SINDI: (*Indicate dream*) Communities throughout the world, sir,
not of Africa alone –

IDI: Is that so?

SINDI: It is an honour, Mr President, to be presented to you thus.

IDI: Good man, good man, what are you?

SINDI: Pakistani, sir.

IDI: I like all Pakistanis. Some are still here because they wanted
Uganda passports of their own volition.

SINDI: I have never before been to your country.

IDI: You would at all times have found it most hospitable –

SINDI: I am a British passport-holding Sudanese resident, sir. I
have lived twenty years in Khartoum.
(*Dream indication ceases. Lights come up.*)

IDI: Dr Fraser you in Nairobi all that time you say?

ANGUS: I was, sir. And my wife had the pleasure to work on the Board of the Kikuyu Karinga Education Association during my term of commission.

IDI: What? . . . That's right . . . That's good . . . Old friend Amos here remember. We King's African Rifles smashed into those tribal groups flirting with what the British called 'Mau Mau'. I don't want Jomo say to me you just white man's imperial black ass man. Jomo think differently from me. But we the same. I'm a brother. Not going to take any lip from American church leader.

ANGUS: Eh . . . who, sir?

IDI: Jomo threw out white American missionary for speaking renegade Russian author. From the pulpit. I do same. I've never read this Solzhenitsyn's rubbish. You read his rubbish?

SINDI: No, sir.

IDI: Most likely Western propaganda in desperate need of a stooge. Author runaway hate his own country love his million Swiss francs he got. And trick him up with Nobel prize award and say he's a martyr. Nothing special about award. Sartre famous French writer turned award down, rubbish. I have a V C . . . here it is . . . Queen didn't give it me. I'm not without pride. I made it. I give it my-self big parade in a silver box. I'm not ashamed. Only the humiliated accept awards any kind. You read this Russian rubbish?

SINDI: No, sir. Definitely.

IDI: Taking no lip from any Christian teacher. You heard of that man Denis Hills Mr Denis Hills silly man: two years ago of the hundred forty-six teachers National Teachers' College, Kampala, there were six black Ugandan teachers, the rest Asians I got nothing against them but, until I come by and see this how can you study from this what chance black Uganda got to learn! And . . . Mr Denis Hills I liked Denis I showed him the law of this country and I advised him about 'Black Nero' whatever that may mean, and writing 'village tyrant' he write, and set him free, give him Mr Callaghan, famous British subject retrieved from black horror camp jail about to be shot in the front page of the *Daily Express*. All this way

Callaghan personal to get Denis, I know Jim well, and in five minutes Hills Mr Hills publishing whole text of the book in a British Sunday paper, and I leave it to James Callaghan who was the Foreign Secretary to say what a dirty trick it is. I'm proven right.

AMOS: Mr President, sir – ?

IDI: I was busy talking.

AMOS: You were, sir.

IDI: Now I ceased.

AMOS: If I may bring to your attention, sir –

IDI: I am Big Daddy 'Dada' Idi Amin and I don't mind it at all. I am Chancellor of Makerere University. Holder of MC, VC, and CBE (Conqueror of the British Empire, that one). Israeli medal of bravery, holder of famous Israeli 'wings' honorary, DSO and full Brigadier-General of all my armies. Nothing serious about that. I laugh at medals. Laugh at fake colonial pomp and glory. Marx said every man should have a few medals keep him cheerful. Commander-in-Chief of my Simba Tigers Ladies' Suicide Battalion. Permanent Deep Diver Boss and water-wings consultant for the Ugandan Army Frogmen Division. Acting-host and chairman for the OAU summit in Kampala, Uganda, 1975. And you are here to see me, well, I give a big welcome!

AMOS: Thank you, sir, I am sure that –

IDI: Anything you want ask.

SINDI: May I put forward the th –

IDI: I hold no hands back.

ANGUS: There is a formal order of precedence with regard to the matters in hand, sir, namely –

IDI: I am a good friend of Britain. Great Britain.

ANGUS: The . . . eh . . . prime consideration, Mr President, for this meeting is to lay down ground rules and preliminary procedure for the Kampala Conference in the forthcoming month.

IDI: I shall have returned from my two meetings first I'll be at the UN Assembly in New York for a crucial vote upon Israel – motion of censure – then I shall be back in Dar-es-Salaam for final Angola Summit jointly make censure of Chinese,

Russian and American imperialist interference in African affairs.

ANGUS: If I may, sir – our function here today is to set out all the itinerary for a joint Uganda / UK settlement on the problem of compensation for those exiled Asians *circa* 1972 and for those business and or registered companies who can right-fully show loss of earnings, fallen ratio of production and considerable economic hardship, particularly in the field of wage structures honoured, meanwhile the firm's production has virtually ceased, and in other fields such as inability to maintain stocks and equipment, the servicing of machinery etc., and the required coal and gas reserves I am thinking particularly of i.e. the mining areas in the south . . . and if I might say so – the normal preferential treatment Uganda has traditionally offered to British mining concessions.

(*Pause.*)

IDI: . . . Yes.

ANGUS: Therefore, sir, I am instructed by senior colleagues at the Defence Ministry taking full cognizance of your enthusiasm for a quick and just settlement to these outstanding matters –

IDI: Uganda always pays its debts.

ANGUS: – and continued relations thus. All forms, all claim forms that is, if I may suggest what has already been laid down in Whitehall, and passed on to your departmental Head of Asian Affairs; if you will recall – HMG has only maintained a token residence at Commission House, Kampala, some-how, in this confusion your departmental Chief did not inform Whitehall that these papers had arrived.

IDI: Sometimes not all things come down the pipe, but I clearly remember my appropriate Minister had already acquainted himself with this paper. I don't know the full reason why he never did reciprocate with your side, or with Commission. House, he should have done, on his own volition, but instead, I think he handed in his formal resignation on board Sudanese Airlines 727 by way of radio contact with my airport staff.

ANGUS: I see, sir.

IDI: I tell you one thing, when any Minister of mine wants to act

fast move quickly you know, by Christ, there is no stopping
them.

ANGUS: And of course, reprinted we find this same Memor-
andum in the House of Commons sessional papers, eh –
papers 196, sir.

IDI: But what do I mind, I bear no beef against any of them, they
go abroad, send wife and kids up front first class take a little
bit of Uganda currency to Switzerland, earn a fat fee from a
capitalist paper saying what a monster I am, what can I do? I
laugh a little. It makes me feel sad. All leaders are betrayed, it
is the sour side of the top.

ANGUS: May I . . . ask here and now . . . sir . . . it is understood
we keep an open-ended arrangement as to how and when the
proposals forthcoming for compensation are to be paid i.e.
there is no hard and fast rule for immediate payment whilst
certain companies may need time to gear up their potential
should these payments be made in a staggered form. I
particularly refer to manufactured goods with production
rundown by the natural course of events and where com-
pensation over a long period i.e. directly related to national
cash flow and Ugandan Government profit-sharing schemes –

IDI: I . . . am following you closely.

ANGUS: If I . . . putting it very plainly, sir . . . eh . . . if such
profits come about with world market currency payments,
the unit of distribution is one very much of mutual benefit to
both countries, or say – the dollar market, euro or IMF or
petro related OPEC currency is swimming in an up-stream
direction, again it is monetary sense to seek joint benefits for
both parties –

IDI: You want to ask me if I like sterling or dollars or marks I like
it all I say.

ANGUS: I need hardly add the rider that – production of manufac-
tured goods accelerates with new government participation
from Ugandan Legislative Powers, and I am sure all such
profits will have all the time in the world to select their
monetary unit of exchange.

IDI: It's called finding the good pig and bringing it on back home,
Dr Fraser.

ANGUS: Well, sir, shall we say we do agree, for openers, on open-ended discussions on friendly terms?

IDI: Of course! That is why we are here!

AMOS: Absolutely! Quite so!

IDI: Why isn't the High Commissioner here? I'd like him to hear that.

AMOS: Sir, I will convey that to the Commissioner this evening.

IDI: Why don't he come here now?

AMOS: I believe he has already expressed his regret. The confusion lay in the fact that he was, as I was, under the impression these preliminary talks would be in the company of your Ministers. Not with you personally –

IDI: My Ministers half the time down town looking up their Shell shares and changing dollars on the black market. I do all the work here.

AMOS: Quite so, sir.

IDI: I do everything I can. I bar them from the golf club until the weekends, I forbid them hiding in other embassies doing unscrupulous talks behind my back, I put the Turkish bath out of bounds until the evening, and if my police see them inside any one of those brothels – all brothels have been banned – their wives are told promptly. I want enlarged specification for each and every claim against the Ugandan Government.

ANGUS: That is laid down in the Government White Paper Memorandum, sir –

IDI: And I need a reciprocal amount of time for Legislative Council appointed business experts to analyse each specification –

ANGUS: Thank you sir . . . no prima facie accountability, all claims subject to full inquiry, reciprocal time allotted, no forms sanctioned without this prior working agreement.

IDI: Now what was it was this 'open-ended discussion on friendly terms' Dr Fraser, you mentioned?

ANGUS: If I may put them in order of precedence –

IDI: That's right –

ANGUS: Item one, sir –

IDI: Item one . . . then . . .

ANGUS: One, channelling funds from UK through the offices of various societies.

IDI: All these things come under open-ended discussion on allied friendly terms?

ANGUS: I'm about to bring to your attention item number one, sir –

IDI: How many items you got written down there?

ANGUS: Channelling funds . . . sir . . . item one, sir . . . various societies both countries unilaterally agree to i.e. – World Council of Health, United Nations Appeal Fund, Church Foundations, Red Cross, Children's Funds and UNESCO.

IDI: I like UNESCO, singers, actors, all famous people running round headless trying improve the lot of those others who want. I liked Red Cross urgent health missions to India and relief famine and flood environmental good deeds and – you got the next item?

ANGUS: Item two – sir . . . eh . . . all concomitant matters relating to cessation . . . of British aid to Uganda –

IDI: I am big friend of UK I want all that aid back, and if I see it coming in the front door Idi pass them back big hallo and gladhand, and I understand Callaghan and the rest see sense; no use cutting off arm of best kith and kin UK got, whole of Africa, long after South Africa sunk under its own sewage, Uganda remain best friend of the Queen.

ANGUS: Further, according to the Memorandum – item three, it will be discussed under close and friendly terms a redefining of the border interests *vis-à-vis* Sudan, Kenya, Zaire and Tanzania.

IDI: Fine by me, want come down and check the borders make sure Uganda friends all round fine by me I'm not ashamed nothing to hide no secret Marxist guerrilla groups attacking Cabenda Dam or training walk in South West Africa, Namibia – what you got there?

ANGUS: Item, sir, four. There will be an informal précis, jointly signed, between heads of signature, namely of course, sir, yourself and our Foreign Minister, a précis of Soviet and Chinese intentions in East Africa.

IDI: Want think whole place crawled up to ears with silent Russians, keep great British public satisfied somebody is still outposting for them in their old colonial world . . . I don't mind. I'm willing to do that for Her Majesty. Why not? What harm done? Only harm I ever see, next British Government in charge turn over whole précis you call it to the CIA . . . what the hell, they say don't they Amos?

AMOS: They do indeed, sir.

IDI: I sign for that one.

ANGUS: Thank you, sir.

IDI: Give me the next number.

ANGUS: Five sir it is item five. There will be an open-ended discussion round table approach on Israeli preoccupation with Sudan. Findings jointly and strictly kept secret, sir.

IDI: I like Israel. Nice people. Only I hate Zionists. Zionists creeping all over Sudan looking for trouble. I ignore them. Israel cannot extend borders where it is common affront to humanity. America knows that. I talk with anyone about Zionists in Sudan. Nothing nobody fear.

ANGUS: Item . . . eh . . . the return of the American Diplomatic Corps to Kampala.

IDI: Very good very welcome there was a little misunderstanding, like them all, bring their wives meet my wives, children get their swimming pools back, dollars always needed, that what so many peoples think back home in England they been brainwashed by the media, I like British media I understand it, but the people don't. And all of a sudden here is Idi Amin with a funny suit on covered in decorations, himself standing in front of the great British laughing public and he is talking about the new ambassador to Ghana to some such place nine out of ten viewers never heard of they don't know anything about Africa except for the fact most of the inhabitants are black length of their general knowledge, and this Idi saying here is the news that America sending Shirley Temple famous film star to Africa as Ambassador . . . and Idi saying this is an outrage because next thing happen before he turn round he standing at Entebbe airport with his medals with the red diplomatic carpet rolled out for US President's new representative in Uganda, and out step off the plane a six-year-old midget in ringlets tapdancing and shaking her curls and shouting about the animal knackers in her soup. And I'm sitting up in my cabinet office with a conductor's stick and all my cabinet of Ministers in the background humming 'The Good Ship Lollipop' instead of 'Stars and Stripes Forever' . . . don't make any mistake . . . I know Shirley Temple is more than six years old now. I like being laughed at. Nice big clean fun. No harm being done me. Lot of harm and ignorance being done famous British audience in their shirt-sleeves rolled up.

ANGUS: Item seven sir . . . the encouragement of tourism in Uganda.

IDI: Welcome it . . . open hands . . . gladly . . . this is the most beautiful place whole East Africa . . . show them round the old native villages . . . the old Kabaka Palace . . . the water-falls. Hunting fishing shooting, wild life, find herbs of all type crocodiles on river trips voyages into the dark forest. And play cards candle-light Ugandan music all the staff in white jackets serving drinks and free mosquito nets those with sensitive skins.

ANGUS: Eight, sir? . . .

IDI: Go ahead, man.

ANGUS: Round-table discussion on a formal visit to the UK, for a second time, at the invitation of Her Majesty's Government.

IDI: Yes, sir.

ANGUS: To be agreed mutually the date and the usual protocol with which, of course, sir, you are familiar.

IDI: With which.

ANGUS: And that, with your permission, Mr President, is the outline of the future open-ended items the next month joint-country meeting here in Kampala.

IDI: Only invitation for a visit to your country which I so love I will accept is one from Her Majesty the Queen herself with whom I already have had the honour of, and I might add, it was she and she alone who recognized my authority here in ten days after the fall of Obote. I am grateful to her for that.

ANGUS: I'm sure you are, sir.

IDI: Oh no I ain't that stupid, you just watch that ass licking, trouble with you Englishers –

ANGUS: I am a Scot, sir – with respect –

IDI: You too damn pleasant. No use sitting around in this world oh how you do nice to meet did you hear the weather report is it cricket and whole damn place from Hong Kong to Panama Canal kicking themselves with laughter. World falling apart and Britain Great British Britain still saying thank you when they boot you down the stairs of the club you once used to own. Now you said to me just a minute you said your superiors from the Defence Ministry same breath you said your superiors are Commonwealth Office what are you Dr Fraser?

ANGUS: I answer to your question, Mr President –

IDI: You CIA – ?

ANGUS: No, sir.

IDI: I remember. My ears tell me. Nobody got two bosses Whitehall one the Defence the other Commonwealth Office –

ANGUS: Naturally sir – in inter-departmental exchange I confer with the Defence Minister. I remain a Commonwealth man, nevertheless. With respect, if I may.

AMOS: Doesn't strike you, sir, as an MI6 man, does he, sir? What?

IDI: I'm not jumping to conclusions, I have an open mind.

ANGUS: What I mean by senior colleagues, I meant – of course, Military Whitehall is always eager to know what we're doing in the Commonwealth Office.

IDI: But I believe you I trust you . . . what was it you said you are?

ANGUS: Liaison Officer for the Assistant Secretary of State, sir: East Africa speciality.

IDI: Very high-up secretary. You are a British permanent secretary?

ANGUS: As permanent as I can make myself, sir.

IDI: I trust you. You are a good man. But . . . I want to know all the details . . . don't want an idiot minister from Kampala come along get it all wrong dates and all and I'm suddenly flying to a big United Nations plenipotentiary talks in New York you ever played American football?

SINDI: Eh . . . no sir.

IDI: Who do we have at the conference here for compensation next month?

AMOS: I think I can best answer that if I may, old chum –

IDI: Very well, *Major* –

AMOS: Sir. I beg your pardon . . . eh . . . to begin with the Commonwealth Office, aside from the Minister, will have two economic advisers, the High Commissioner here and the Assistant Under-Secretary of State, Dr Fraser's senior, and at least one separate man for each of the broad and friendly based items on the White Paper Memorandum which Dr Fraser has already outlined. This will make a separate joint committee if you will, to be countered on your side, sir, with respect, with your own group of experts –

IDI: How many men?

AMOS: Well . . . I'd say HMG will have to provide a per head count before arrival *pro rata* the necessaries. No extra fat on the diplomatic bag. What were you thinking of, Mr President, in view of – ?

IDI: Nothing . . . nothing at all . . . really.

AMOS: I'll telephone London tonight sir, or even catch the over-night bag Dar-es-Salaam flight –

IDI: Not important at all – I like the Nile Hotel to have the correct number of rooms available.

AMOS: Qu . . . quite.

IDI: Popular hotel the Nile.

AMOS: Sir?

IDI: Most my Ministers tucking away six-course breakfast eight o'clock mornings until I banned them from here too.

AMOS: Absolutely.

IDI: Bedsheets . . . hot water . . . air-conditioning . . . piped TV . . . colour . . .

AMOS: I will see to it HMG provide per head count details.

IDI: How many Asians coming along next month?

SINDI: With your permission Mr President –

IDI: Yes yes what the use of talking like this when you are come here to collect money from me and I am ready to meet you and my bank is open with all its wealth you still talk about permission. I am a friend of the world.

SINDI: There . . . there will be four of us with a complement of secretarial staff. Two men from the United Nations Board of Inquiry into the plight of Asians based in Geneva, myself and a Swahili-speaking international lawyer from London.

IDI: Is he Asian?

SINDI: Although Pakistani by birth, he carries a British Indian dual nationality –

IDI: He ever been here?

SINDI: He has never set foot on Ugandan soil.

IDI: He is Indian?

SINDI: With respect he is British, in his capacity as spokesman for Asian compensation, sir.

IDI: I got more letters from Delhi drawerful stack high from Mr J. S. Mehta, additional Secretary of the Indian Ministry of External Affairs, he say there are 1,500 newly impoverished Indians I've thrown out, I write back and says yes quite true how much? He write back he don't believe I'm ready to pay. I write back say the cheque book in my hand. He write back say no money in Bank of Uganda. CIA inform him bunch of lies, it never stop with these Indians never do. And British newspapers tell lies to their bourgeois readers that every night I sit at home and study my Who's Who of black Africa titled *Who Dat?* I got news for the great British public, Africa full of a thousand million black souls still bleeding from those colonial wounds. You like the view from my window? No barbed wire on my window. You don't see any Mahdi gunmen with automatic rifles body-guarding me here this is a peaceful place. You seen my cartoons? . . . Seen – Trogg, Cummings (Cummings mad vindictive fascist dog I like him he is honest I have him in my house for a cup of tea), *Private Eye* famous monthly weekly of the British Isles obscene witticisms. Garland (who he?) don't know him, Emmwood, Heath (another relation I suppose), Scarfe, Marc . . . all the top cartoonists . . . all drawn me . . . What do you think Amos?

AMOS: Quite disgraceful British propaganda.

IDI: Smother the English with big bad Idi, smother the English with violent revolution in Portugal (five killed in one year that what they call violent BBC propaganda) smother everyone with what they call World Service smother the public with revolution all over the world in every country except the place where it matters, where it should be shown, in Belfast, seaside capital of Irish Republic don't belong to Britain anyway, each week nobody say ten men women and children die ten of them and the bombings and the murders oh no got to hide it all away behind big Dada Amin laughter, no one mention fact that America retain nuclear submarine bases in Ireland official secret word from Washington to London don't get out of Ireland, secret Kissinger Zionist talk about Ireland becoming the Cuba of off-shore Europe second Cuba for the Russians and hundreds of plain clothes SAS army thugs first they shoot a Catholic then they go down the road and shoot a Protestant then a war starts in the road and the army turns round to Whitehall says there you are what did we say we need more men here to keep conflict under control . . . Poor Big Daddy what he done to deserve all this. Everybody get bad publicity some of the time. I get it all the time. Then I said something nice about Hitler. Adolf Hitler German Führer of the united German peoples before the war ended in 1945, European war that is. I said something nice about him (there may not be so many nice things you can say about him) all of a sudden what I see I am saying in the papers – 'Hitler was right to burn six million Jews.' Who was right? I said that? I ask you, you look at those cartoons you read that sort of nonsense silly bugger say so what we in the King's African Rifles used to call 'tommyrot'. Would the President of the OAU run around shouting about burning six million any peoples? Everything I've done! You have to understand my sense of humour, smile a bit, kid along the white man a bit, I have twenty children of my own . . . five wives . . . one just dead . . . one new one just recent . . .

would you marry your daughter to a man like that who just burnt six million of them?

AMOS: Splendid stuff!

ANGUS: I wonder if I may . . . return to my series of programme points for the coming top-level meeting here, Mr President?

IDI: That is right.

ANGUS: If I check them down, detail by detail, can I take that as your assurance?

IDI: You can.

ANGUS: (*Files out on knee*) This list . . . of companies is complete and, though there might indeed be deletions or voluntary withdrawals of claim, there will assuredly be no further additions.

IDI: I understand.

ANGUS: These are claims for UK firms seeking lawful compensation in excess of £100 million.

IDI: Uganda pays.

ANGUS: Sir?

IDI: Bank of Uganda pays.

ANGUS: I –

IDI: All debts to be honoured world wide. This is an honest country.

ANGUS: Of course, sir, naturally –

IDI: I pick up this phone here – and at the other end of the line is my Manager of the Bank of Uganda –

AMOS: Eh – *President*, sir.

IDI: My Manager – nobody is encouraged much in this country to raise themselves to the level of President or Brigadier, unless I approve the say-so. I ring him up I say go down the basement and open up the bomb-proof Swiss-installed gates Idi your President coming in for the big handout and he goes running down those stairs like I was a pedigree cross between Al Capone and Jack the Ripper reason you get no specialist murderers like Jack the Ripper in Africa creeping about in the misty London streets knocking off prostitutes and cutting out their vaginas reason being there is no pressures here like the olden days in Great Britain you heard of Jack the Ripper Mr Sindi?

SINDI: Yes, sir.

ANGUS: May I commence, with respect, with the firm of Smith Mackenzie Ltd; a claim for £406,000 against Uganda for loss of trade due to the sudden dismissal of ninety per cent of their staff during the Economic Year of Uganda – ?

IDI: Uganda pay.

ANGUS: Mackinon and Bros, £229,000.

IDI: We pay.

ANGUS: Wigglesworth Co. Ltd, £778,000.

IDI: Any sum over half a million sterling claimed against Uganda, while I accept most probably, this claim here, waiting on the most intense and vigorous Ugandan investigation by my experts into this claim, any sum over half . . . paid out of the fifty-one per cent Ugandan Government stake, the relative profits from such will pay over a period of twenty years.

ANGUS: Ralli Bros, £800,000.

IDI: Don't know them.

SINDI: Asian cloth merchants, sir, and factories for cotton yarn processing, and plastic fibre marrying processes.

IDI: I am not unjust. Asian or otherwise. Why should I attack Asians. They will get their money.

ANGUS: Mitchell Cotts Co. Ltd, claim of £490,000.

IDI: Fine.

ANGUS: Jos. Hansen Ltd, £169,000.

IDI: Bank pays.

ANGUS: African Mercantile and East Coast Marine Corps, £224,000.

IDI: Yes. Bank pays in Ugandan currency except where I stipulate as otherwise. For all claims.

ANGUS: Twentsche Overseas Trading Corps, £355,000.

IDI: Yes. All German and allied Asian businesses get their money.

ANGUS: Brooke Bond, £900,000. Destroyed stock on 1971 books.

IDI: Famous British tea bags with little holes. Amos?

AMOS: Quite, absolutely.

ANGUS: Barclays Overseas (East African Division), a sum of £6,480,000.

IDI: That is quite separate. All that is frozen assets. All will be released in the appropriate currencies they are held in, or exchange units with a guarantee from Bank of Uganda. I am not a fool, I would like Barclays men come here and justify how many millions they saved by putting all this six million down in their London city accountings as losses against taxation – cut that item from your list, please, Doctor.

ANGUS: Certainly certainly. Now . . .

IDI: Then this all-important meeting come to a close.

(IDI *strides purposefully towards the door.* FRASER *makes an effort to pluck up courage as they all abruptly stand for* IDI.)

ANGUS: . . . Sir! . . .

IDI: We all finished now.

ANGUS: If I may, sir –

IDI: All talking done.

ANGUS: I –

AMOS: If sir, you could see your way to just one or two final points which, though of course being minor, the Under-Secretary when he arrives next month will have prepared notes on . . . Sir . . . ?

IDI: What more notes he got?

(ANGUS *and* AMOS *exchange looks.* AMOS *gently takes* IDI'*s arm and strolls with him across to the desk.*)

AMOS: May I as an old friend . . . Field Marshal, sir . . . the whole question of aid is in Uganda's national interest –

IDI: Uganda don't need aid. Uganda got the help of all African black nations got Libya and USSR and Saudi Arabia and Palestine Liberation –

AMOS: I think Dr Fraser has a further point on this – if you will –

ANGUS: Sir, HMG has since the expulsion of Ugandan Asians reduced original aid in the region of annual three million pounds sterling to something barely accommodating wages for British National teachers through the Ministry of Overseas Development, and yet there is still a basic imbalance between the bi-national trade – standing at, in the order of, some twenty million pounds sterling value into UK against seven millions imported into Uganda –

IDI: Nobody give anything away three quarters of that larger sum belongs to private trading profit between British-owned companies, what Uganda see out of that precious little but a pittance tax –

ANGUS: I'd also like to remind the Field Marshal that some nine million francs annually form an EEC Central Loan Subsidy to East Africa which UK makes an additional eighteen per cent commitment fee towards.

IDI: We done now?

ANGUS: I only wish to explore these basic facts, sir.

IDI: They explored now.

ANGUS: And you accept, generally speaking, these facts are correct, sir?

IDI: Correct, correct. I go now.

ANGUS: . . . Sir! . . .

IDI: What you have now?

ANGUS: One positive final item will be on the Under-Secretary's agenda –

IDI: It the final one.

ANGUS: Being, an attempt should be made to outline a bilateral agreement on the general safety of UK nationals in Uganda, there are . . . it stands at the most recent count some three hundred eighty-six UK passport immigrant cardholders. A number of missionaries working north at Mbale, and at Masaka, and at Lake Edward, and certain medical people, who receive their salaries through the Catholic Fund for Overseas Development.

(*He slumps in the chair behind the desk. The impatience has given way to a cumbrous drowsiness.*)

IDI: You come to see me. And I am here. Now you have finished all this and we set about the business with my Cabinet. First I talk to them. Then they talk to you. Then all the Under-Secretaries of State meet next month I could be called away in an instant on my travels. What are we saying what we doing here? For we should make a joint statement announce initial intentions to lay down procedure for big meeting –

ANGUS: With respect, this is precisely –

IDI: And tell the world whole world waiting for genuine positive action in the face of many crises what we say?

SINDI: If I may point out – I am not sure Dr Fraser being an Englishman can see it so clearly – this is an attempt to detail exactly the British commitment to Uganda, and to account for every aspect of British interests in order that both countries exactly reciprocate true understanding.

IDI: You write it down . . . An intelligent man . . . Intelligent Indian. I like Indians. This top-drawer level meeting terminated.

AMOS: Sir!

IDI: You all need long cold shower in the hotel. Is the tap running?

AMOS: Sir!

IDI: Tomorrow big treat I'll take you up the Nile show the crocs no show the crocs you you will not be afraid because I'll be with you I'll show all my military planning campaign to utterly destroy centre of Tel Aviv in one counter-stroke.

ANGUS: It would be a fascinating experience, Mr President.

IDI: Must understand I like Jews I wear this Star of David top Israeli medal I respect them the greatest fighters on earth. Goodbye.

(IDI *cordially shakes* ANGUS *and* AMOS *by the hand. And* SINDI, *who is the last to leave.*)

IDI: (*Indicate dream*) No you . . . you can come back.

SINDI: (*Indicate dream*) Me, sir?

IDI: I want to show I have the most cordial willing to spend more time than with any other particularly those Britishers civil service gobblegook I like Britishers but it is the Indians I must show my new face to. The kind face. I have no complaint. I let all things pass. Then I hear that the British Government complaining ten million pound a week sterling smuggled out of the country to Jamaica and West Indies and Kingston and India all sent back home and I am laughing. Where did you think all the Uganda currency went up to 1972? It went out through the Post Office go down there any Saturday morning you like I take you I could have shown you what is in those fat envelopes? All this money going out to India and Pakistan and the whole cash-flow currency of Uganda bleeding a death.

SINDI: If I may point out, sir that —

IDI: I heard all that before. But I have forgiven. You are forgiven. You are a friend. Come in peace here. I'll show you my children beside the swimming pool. All Indians clever and resourceful. You heard of Prophet John? The great prophet of my country? He come from Lugazi. My mother loved a Muslim greatly from there. And I was born in Koboko West Nile Province. My father was Kakwe. My mother was a Lugbara. She ran away from him with me. She went from one barracks to another, always with me, from Jinja to Buikwe to Lugazi. I could speak Luganda and Kiswahili and Aruan Sudanic. And I was the heavyweight champion of the British army. Prophet John come to me, he say he can read into the future. He can see into the other parts of the future where no one else can penetrate. I ask him Prophet what going to pass? With me? He say you are going to die, and a hero and a national Africa all African hero you'll become. So, I pick you out from the others because it is necessary to show this hand of friendship broad big as Africa even to an Indian. I don't hate them I think they work hard but they must work for the country in which they thrive and not against it. You wouldn't like all Bagandese take over rice production in India and send it all back to Masaka? My dream is, say the Prophet, Idi's dream — I will know the hour of my end and the exact minute and who done it. You like Agatha Christie novels?

SINDI: Mr President, I have a message for you from a number of old friends of yours outside of Uganda — Muhammed Hussein, and Colonels M. Arach, A. Langoya, Akwango, Ojok, Abwala, Ayumi, Ekirring, P. Obol, O. Ogwal; the soldiers and friends of Lugbara, the men and women of Mbarara, former Prime Minister of Uganda, Kiwanua; Vice-Chancellor of Makerere University, Kalimuzo; Governor of the Bank of Uganda, Mubiru; the Chief-Justice of Uganda, Benedicto Kiwanuka and Archbishop Luwum.

IDI: All these men are missing or dead.

SINDI: It is their message to you, sir —

(SINDI *holds a small pistol in his hands. He stands close up to* IDI *and grips the butt with both hands for firmness. He holds it steadily*

and as far away from his eyes as he can. SINDI *pulls the trigger. No percussion.*
Blackout. Sound of loud breathing. Lights up. IDI *is in his cot bed. The dreamer is sleeping.*)

ACT TWO
Kampala Real

Jinja bungalow. It is an untidy front room. Ceiling fan rotates. Stick furnishings. Cabinet files. Impression of litter and haste.

MAJOR GEORGE 'AMOS' TODD *enters in full uniform. He sits behind a desk and lays out his papers from a portfolio. He takes off his hat and rings a stand-bell before him.*

Shouting and shoving from outside. A manacled 'ANGUS FRASER' *wearing filthy light clothes with a couple of days' stubble is shoved into the room. The door slams behind him. The time is as close to the present as we can assume.*

AMOS: . . . Ah, there you are. Good morning.

ANGUS: Good?

AMOS: Here we are, at last.

ANGUS: Where . . . are we?

AMOS: First of all shall we take things easily . . . first steps et cetera . . . explore the terrain if you will . . .

ANGUS: Who in hell are you?

AMOS: To begin with, I'm British . . . eh . . . set your mind at rest.

ANGUS: I want to use a telephone right away –

AMOS: Aah . . .

(He holds up the mouthpiece of the machine 'ANGUS' *grabs at on the desk. No sound.)*

. . . Dead as a door-nail, what? Only phone you ever find working here belongs to the Wabenzi; no sound at all, what?

ANGUS: I demand . . .

AMOS: Let's sit down shall we? Little more civilized. I'm sorry about the . . . eh . . . cuff-links. I did request – but trouble with finding the key – and Towilli is not here, he is up

country chasing through bush looking for an idiot Asian
accidentally come over the Kenya border and says he lost his
way, poor sod, where were we?

ANGUS: I demand help. Who are you from?

AMOS: I think you'll find . . . I'm the one responsible for most of
the questioning here.

ANGUS: Why am I here?

AMOS: Start at starters shall we –

ANGUS: Are you in a position to help me?

AMOS: According to all this tommyrot written down – worst
typing since Caterham School Corps tents and provisions
inventory.

ANGUS: Who is Towilli?

AMOS: (*More to himself and the papers*) I'm ready, are you?

ANGUS: And most important of all – where am I?

AMOS: I am George 'Amos' Todd. Major. Uganda has been my
stamping-ground for many years. And I have the benefit of
direct communication with the Ruling Defence Council in
Kampala.

ANGUS: Where am I?

AMOS: This is the bungalow home of Superintendent Ali Towilli.
We are in Jinja which is, as you know, forty miles north-east
of Entebbe.

ANGUS: Ali who?

AMOS: Superintendent Towilli is the boss-man of the State Re-
search Bureau of Uganda. It was formerly a part of the Public
Safety Unit. As I say he is not –

ANGUS: You are British?

AMOS: Yes, indeed. Very proud.

ANGUS: But acting in what capacity?

AMOS: My orders were to come here and explore the situation,
direct orders from Ruling Defence Council. What you mean
is – Britain HMG has no direct diplomatic link with Uganda
but the Government House office keeps three secretaries at
the French Consulate –

ANGUS: Then let me speak to the French Consul!

AMOS: I think you ought to know that President the Field Mar-
shal Amin has already given audience to M. Pierre Renard,

from the French Consulate, and M. Renard recommended me to see you first. Although I have no direct link with HMG I am free to pass on all matters British as it were to the highest level in Kampala. Now . . . if you'll bear with me . . . (*From the documents*) Your name is –

ANGUS: Greville William Allnutt.

AMOS: Your name is . . . eh – Angus Fraser.

ANGUS: The name is Greville William Allnutt.

AMOS: Eh – Dr Angus Fraser.

ANGUS: I am referred to as a doctor. Indeed, I use it deliberately, in my business practice. As Dr G. W. Allnutt.

AMOS: I see.

ANGUS: Clearly, there has been some monumental blunder.

AMOS: You say you are not Dr Angus Fraser?

ANGUS: Allnutt is the name. A patronymic which, along with equally ancient designations as Clutterbuck, Bigglesthwaite or anything ending with Stein, seems to produce a wave of adolescent humour on a level not unadjacent to lavatory graffiti . . .

AMOS: Nevertheless, you are a 'doctor'?

ANGUS: When I left UK to work in Tanzania three years ago, I was a qualified veterinary surgeon. In due course, by a series of good luck and blind judgement, I accepted a government post analysing cattle vaccines, specializing in certain areas of immunology, and the title stuck. It added a useful bonus to my salary.

AMOS: And eh . . . you insist you are not Dr Angus Fraser?

ANGUS: I do not know such a name, I have never assumed such a name, and you will see from my passport, I see it is there before – indeed I am G. W. of the funny-haha surname.

AMOS: Ah : . . umm, quite.

ANGUS: On a fairly run-of-the-mill passport bearing Her Britannic Majesty's reasonable request that I may be allowed to pass freely without let or hindrance, even, dare I mention it, be afforded such assistance and protection as may be necessary wherever I might find myself.

AMOS: The ambiguities have not escaped me, sir.

ANGUS: I have been locked up downstairs, in what I can only take for a concreted pig-bunker, for two nights, without light or food, and briefly I was allowed a drink half an hour before they brought me up to you.

AMOS: Yes well . . . for pretty brutal but obvious reasons, they don't have many actual cells in this part of town. Principally, simple truth is they don't waste much time with any bod they pick up v. quick goodnight Irene and a bathe in the river Kioga. You seem pretty certain I must say . . .

ANGUS: About what?

AMOS: Certain you are not Angus Fraser.

ANGUS: Greville is the name. I am married to a nice lady born in the Potteries, born Alice Chandley, mother of two boys of mine, George and Edward, and for eight years we lived happily in number four, Edgemount Close, Hereford.

AMOS: And you insist you are as it says here you are – one G. W. –

AMOS: ⎫
⎬ – Allnutt.
ANGUS: ⎭

ANGUS: My mother's maiden name Tuppersley, she and my father William, were married 14 December 1927, Church of All Souls, Parish of Shrub End, Worcestershire Diocese, and, sad as I am the passport does not include these details, I won a Deacon Andrews Scholarship to Lucton Preparatory School at the age of ten.

AMOS: But you are a doctor?

ANGUS: Later, in my advanced teens, I failed to gain a selection for the science Tripos at St David's University, Lampeter, and I enrolled with desperation in an advanced students' course of animal surgery at Burford, Oxon; a venture jointly financed by the late great Lord Nuffield and a dog biscuit manufacturer who had retired to Cap Grasse on the French Med.

AMOS: All to the good . . . old fellow . . . I must soldier through all this nevertheless. You have no address in London?

ANGUS: My wife and I share a stucco white cement rendered flat-roofed community apartment by the sea, north of Dar-es-Salaam, at Tanga, built by the Chinese ten years ago for workers on the state iron-ore smelting plant. I live between this said plant and a palm oil refinery, at a humble address, titled PO Box 900, Avenue Chou en-Lai, and I last visited London to see Danny Kaye at the London Palladium in 1951.

AMOS: You have never been a First Secretary to the Foreign and Commonwealth Office?

ANGUS: No I have never had such a posting.

AMOS: Never worked as direct liaison with the East African Advisory Board?

ANGUS: True.

AMOS: With direct responsibility to the office of the Assistant Under-Secretary of State – ? Commonwealth Office?

ANGUS: Absolutely.

AMOS: You . . . eh . . . have lived in Nairobi a number of years –

ANGUS: I have not.

AMOS: Your wife has maintained a teaching post there –

ANGUS: She has not.

AMOS: All in all, you insist you are who you say you are, and anything said to the contrary is false?

ANGUS: I'm glad you have come round to seeing it my way.

AMOS: Well, sir, I have to tell you that this makes it very difficult for all parties concerned.

ANGUS: It does, does it? Why?

AMOS: If all this information I have here can be firmly disproved, things might go more smoothly; but you have no idea of the detail and surveillance every UK citizen is undergoing at this time in this country. Why . . . were you seen loitering outside Entebbe airport three days ago?

ANGUS: I was flying East African Airlines from Lusaka, where I had attended a conference of animal-feed bacteriologists, with particular concern for new enzootics created by grain cargo deficiencies. I had planned to stop off at Entebbe to meet friends. If I did not find them at the airport, they'd leave a car for me to pick up. No soon as I landed, I was told the crew had been arrested, reasons not stated.

AMOS: You were seen driving a green BMW with Uganda nameplates six hours after passing through customs.

ANGUS: I have friends at Jinja. Naomi and Karl Murchison. Karl is a Dutch Reform Church missionary based here. His wife told me to find the car keys under the off-side wheel hub outside the airport where Karl had left them, and drive out she said to Jinja. When I arrived at the mission house, I was told that Mrs Murchison had been taken away. And that I must wait for her. The boy did not stop to talk. He ran off.

AMOS: You were not aware of the banning of all cars for the time being?

ANGUS: Maybe I was – but I had no choice – what other way was there for me to get to Jinja? Walk forty miles at night with a suitcase?

AMOS: Mrs Murchison has not been located anywhere. There is no evidence that she even spoke to you. Nor is there any boy from the mission house.

ANGUS: The boy was Catholic Bantu, I think called – Bumali.

AMOS: Why were you staying at this empty mission house when you were picked up by officers of the State Research Bureau?

ANGUS: I was silly enough to wait around to see if either Naomi or Karl might return. Or the boy. Nobody did. I then took it into my own hands to drive the BMW back to the airport hoping the plane would take me on to Dar. That is, if it was still there. I had no means of getting in touch with anyone – the phone mysteriously packed up – nobody arrived – and these hoodlums in khaki stopped me. At gun-point. Took away all cash I had on me. Emptied the car of petrol. And drove me pillion motorbike to here at night.

AMOS: Back to Jinja.

ANGUS: And I know nothing more. It is a simple story. And I wish only for a telephone which works that I might speak to my wife and boys, explain where I am, and, hopefully provide myself with the wherewithal to get out of here, whatever it takes.

AMOS: I am afraid I am also requested to ask you what properties you own freehold or otherwise in Uganda?

ANGUS: None.

AMOS: Have you . . . ever . . . conspired to assassinate the President of Uganda?

ANGUS: No I have not.

AMOS: Have you ever met with or conversed with any Asians

you may know, no matter how brief the connection, who themselves have shown keenness to assassinate the President of Uganda?

ANGUS: No.

AMOS: I have a . . . further . . . item . . . here; yes – on Thursday morning last you were seen talking to an Asian, on a street corner, beside the Chrysler-Africa billboard? Jinja south, Gadaphi Market Place. You handed him certain papers?

ANGUS: I have no recollection.

AMOS: There is indisputable evidence for this.

ANGUS: I just don't give a wild damn if the United Nations saw it, it means nothing to me. Nor should it to you, whoever you are.

(AMOS *stands*.)

AMOS: This meeting is closed. I'll take you back to the cell. I will get back to you as soon as I can.

ANGUS: Is that all? All you've got to say!

AMOS: Old man, thank your stars – at least you've got me.

(*The light changes.*
At the back of a hangar-like wall stands a Bell 600 helicopter. IDI *sits inside the glass dome. The crackle from a transmitter stabs the air. It is his own voice on Radio Uganda.* AMOS *smartly approaches and taps on the glass wing door.* IDI *gestures for him to sit beside him.*)

AMOS: . . . Mr President, sir?

IDI: Come and sit down . . . Command Post full of howling wives talking about Swiss Bank Accounts and numbered vault boxes . . . I tell them I haven't any and I tell you the truth and not one of them believes me. Women! They have been reading French magazines, always think the President of this or that has got a box of gold. I'm no common thief from my own land. What box of gold?

AMOS: Very fine machine this, Mr President.

IDI: That's right. I got sixty-five Bell 600 copters and no gasoline to fly them with, even if I had gasoline I couldn't trust four Russian-trained pilots to switch on the windscreen wipers, let alone take it up.

AMOS: Unusual . . . eh . . . place to meet in at your request, of course, sir.

IDI: What's the use . . . no use meeting in the Security Council Room, or at the Command Post, I've locked the Cabinet up in the Command Post and I've told the entire chiefs of staff to stay in that Cabinet room until they devise a system of government which stops spreading thousands of leaflets demanding my resignation and other actions of public revolt against me, in person me, because as I tell them, they are doing exactly what those revisionist Zionist Western capitalists want. Play into their hands. Put back Africa, black Africa hundred years my resignation would.

AMOS: Yes sir.

(*This new* IDI *is a quiet figure. Softly spoken and heavy and there is a certain sadness. A clumsy egg walking tongue-toed quality. The rambler of the dream is quite different from this heavy and ponderous man.*)

IDI: All history books tell the story of millions of blacks in Africa, untold in their numbers, century after century, blacks burnt, blacks hung, blacks genocide, black slaver-ships, black sweated labour, half the gold, half the diamonds, half the iron-ore, entire black continent ripped off and they white hypocrites in London or Paris say to me, 'Big bad black boy, you killed couple of thousand dissidents, you are worse than Hitler.'

AMOS: With respect, sir – I have interviewed the Britisher from the plane. The doctor.

IDI: He's a spy.

AMOS: Difficult to pin it on him.

IDI: Can be done.

AMOS: Legally, lawfully, that is, sir.

IDI: He's a British doctor. Secret spy from Commonwealth Office. He is Angus Fraser.

AMOS: Sir, he claims to be Greville William Allnutt.

IDI: No. I know he is Fraser.

AMOS: I am in the dark here – sir – who is this Fraser?

IDI: He says he is a secretary, East African Advisory Board, Commonwealth Office, London. But he is not.

AMOS: Who then is he?

IDI: He is this man you have here in the disguise of the other one.

AMOS: Other one?

IDI: Fraser one.

AMOS: I don't see the connecting link as it were, why should Fraser want to be Allnutt or Allnutt pretend not to be Fraser?

IDI: And this other one – this Indian – you've seen him?

AMOS: He is being brought in, sir.

IDI: He has to be brought in alive.

AMOS: I have heard nothing to the contrary.

IDI: The other one, the Asian Indian one, is called Baru – Sindi Baru.

AMOS: Quite.

IDI: It doesn't matter what name he says he is, he is Baru. And he has been seen talking to the other one the British one.

AMOS: And the one knows the other, sir, is that it?

IDI: Years ago, after we changed King's African Rifles to Uganda Rifles, and Iain Grahame. You remember Iain, Major?

AMOS: I remember Iain Grahame well, sir. Last I heard of him he was on British television putting up a spirited defence on your behalf to the British public at large.

IDI: Iain came from Sandhurst.

AMOS: Best training ground for future men on earth, sir.

IDI: My son my son . . . Gamal . . . Gamal Abdal – Nazzar Ja-Wami I wanted to please the British give them something to look up to and send the boy there but first he is a Muslim and that is not Sandhurst.

AMOS: Now . . . sir . . . about these two men – with the separate names –

IDI: Years ago after King's African Rifles became Uganda Rifles, I was told by Prophet John, told me when I would die and who would be the killer and I never did believe him I told him the old fool he was. Until I . . . had this dream.

AMOS: Dream, sir – ?

IDI: No. Dreams. They are many now. They come back and it is the same names – these Britishers and Asian there, same names, talking about compensation for Asians who bled my country white, and then the dreams do not go away. I see this man who kills me. And his accomplice. Beside you, there, too.

AMOS: I assuredly pray I do not appear beside them sir –

IDI: You in the dream.

AMOS: Oh no sir, not me, sir.

IDI: But I forgive you for that. I know my Amos like I know Baruch-Bar-Lev, in Israel. I trust rank and honesty. And I like what you are for me. You are British Great British Amos Queen's British as it was when we had old Baganda days. Now . . . British race of washing-machine rats. Receiver of Western dumping little island. England become everybody's roast pig on a spit because everyone know the proud note is all the international strength the island got. British people think they have no censorship entire press stained with secrecy no one wants to tell the British public that gold now become totally devalued because Portugal, only country left with vast gold and no international debts wants to sell it over the counter, little Britishers with fat sums invested in South Africa aren't told that. Suddenly the Queen's sceptre not worth the nickel. In the street Western capitalist nations still dreaming diamonds and gold future contain nothing like that at all bourgeois rubbish future contain continent of Africa rich and black future contain continent of South America Marxist and rich nothing else inbetween but decay and rot and do you know how many Scots landowners own the entire length of the River Tweed great River Tweed through Berwickshire – ?

AMOS: No, sir, I don't.

IDI: My information is – twenty-two.

AMOS: Absolutely shocking piece of information, sir.

IDI: Now I have had this dream again . . . and they kill me. Now, they the British are hunting me down. Those whom I have given the most favours to. Factories, employment, friendship against the advice of all my Sudan and Libyan friends – you go back to those men – you find their real names – I don't want to put those Mafuta Mingi men put on them. I don't want them degooded. Don't want them treated like common *magendo* trash, but you find out where their friends,

and what guns they got, who is financing this? Remember
Amos you, too, were in these dreams. But you had nothing
to do with it, you are a Sandhurst man. I will tell you by
phone where and when to meet. I must have the truth out of
them.

(AMOS *climbs out from the Bell and smartly salutes.*)

AMOS: Sir!

(*Jinja bungalow of* TOWILLI's. *This time there is debris and chaos
from a ransacking job. Everything is strewn.* MAJOR AMOS *tries to
clear the floor for a chair. The desk is upturned. Above his head the
electric fan has stopped.* AMOS *pauses amidst the chaos. The
tiredness of the day.* AMOS *takes out a coloured neckerchief from his
pocket. He wipes the perspiration from the back of his collar. He
appears to have stood there waiting for a long time, but it has all been
seconds. Banging and shoving and a half-naked* 'SINDI' *is brought
through the door. He is chained. There is blood and contusion on
him:* AMOS *barely looks up.*

'SINDI' *stands shocked. Waiting for the door to slam behind him.
During this scene a flashlight bright as a lighthouse reflector bursts
through the window-panes. It sidles backwards and is then switched
off.*)

AMOS: Right . . . according to my instructions we will have little
trouble with you. You have good English?

SINDI: Oh yes, sir, Major sir.

AMOS: Report says you have good command of Somali, and a
smatter of Nubian West Nile dialect?

SINDI: Yes sir, I do.

AMOS: How come?

SINDI: I work for Jallaquar, one-arm bandit East African con-
cession, Kenya, Sudan, Uganda, Tanzania, Zambia. All fruit
machine collection and gift trade is authorized through the
company's official carrier. I have been a senior carrier with
Jallaquar since 1968.

AMOS: Oh, yes.

SINDI: I understand I was arrested and brought here on a case of
mistaken identity nothing about which I know at all.

AMOS: You were picked up by the State Research Bureau on the strict authority of the Superintendent Towilli, Ali Towilli.

SINDI: I have not spoken with Towilli.

AMOS: At this stage of events, nor have I. I believe Towilli himself has been put into detention in the Nile Hotel under suspicion of mutiny. And he is the head of police as you might say.

SINDI: I don't see how I can be detained then, if —

AMOS: Look, laddie — the whole point of this matter is not to detain you, it is to let you go free. You were interrogated at four a.m. this morning by senior members of the Kampala Command Post HQ?

SINDI: I was informally introduced to six Arab gentlemen, who claimed they were personal staff to the President. They made their presence felt in various parts of my anatomy. Since then I have been sick, frequently, coughed blood, and lost all feeling in my right arm. My ears maintain a peculiar feeling also.

AMOS: Appears to have a certain humorous approach.

SINDI: I know Uganda and love it well, and the people here; what has happened to me is not so very different from hundreds of others accidentally caught up in this situation; I particularly refer to Kenyans caught on or near the border, and arbitrarily dealt with in the most vicious manner. Fortunately for myself, I do carry all correct papers of identification, my British passport and my Sudanese citizenship.

AMOS: Everything tidy and neatly in place . . . an answer for almost everything . . . what are you a Paki?

SINDI: I am a Baluchi Muslim. My parents were killed in the massacres after partition in 1948, when the Muslim League could not support those in the north-west against the merciless Hindu onslaught. In fact, what Urdu I could speak then I have utterly put aside. I am British and Sudanese, above all I am Muslim.

AMOS: Highly articulate . . . born Pakistan . . . professes Muslim faith or ideology. Parents killed by Hindu nationalists after UK get out. Right you are!

(*Searchlight flicks across windows. A rotation, it would appear from its regularity.*)

SINDI: Why are we being flashed like this . . . ?

AMOS: Sonny . . . that I cannot give an exact reply to . . . it may be, as this is the house of the police superintendent, and as he himself is under lock and key, there must be those factions who consider anyone caught inside the building highly suspect. Including me. Are you aware of the situation out there in the streets? No petrol. Little electricity. Food down to bananas and Red Cross stores' dried milk, and every office and bank in Kampala is closed. All four borders to the country are blocked. And you ask me about flashing lights! I don't wish to unnerve your tough little Paki shell but this is a state of chronic emergency.

SINDI: I do not understand who I am speaking to; if you might be so kind as to enlighten me?

AMOS: I am a mere liaison officer between all British passport holders in Uganda and the *pro tem*. UK Office in the French Consulate. It is my sad duty to keep any one – Britons or blue passport wogs carrying this – (*Holds up the passport*) like yourself the hell out of this country because it is *pro tem*. and very *tem*. at that about to allow the shit to hit the fan at the highest diplomatic level. Now . . . just what were you doing driving that motorbike through the Kenya border up towards Jinja?

SINDI: I was lost. There was not a single light at night. All road signs had been smashed down.

AMOS: Where were you intended for?

SINDI: I had an appointment with a spare parts retailer, German-based firm of Schweikers Son Ltd, at Busia, but all road signs were down. I then decided to head on inland when I knew from Southern Cross star light that Jinja lay west at the angle of ninety degrees, and I had a fruit machine plastic component assembly gentleman to see, who had offered high-margin deductions if we considered his apparatus. In fact, it would seem, his type of plastic has an asbestos base which allows for considerable strength –

AMOS: In all this, you had no idea or thought that the entire country might lie on the verge of flames?

SINDI: Sir, with respect, I am a business agent, and my work

takes me through six or seven East African countries, revol-
utions and uprisings need not interfere with the commercial
progress.

AMOS: You say so?

SINDI: With the greatest respect, sir, I do, sir.

(AMOS *leans over his papers on the desk and writes wearily.*)

AMOS: Full name?

SINDI: Isaid Dem Ala-Messid Jalli.

AMOS: Nationality?

SINDI: Sudanese joint UK citizenship.

AMOS: Place of birth?

SINDI: Shikarpur, Baluchistan; West Pakistan.

AMOS: Present occupation?

SINDI: . . . Sales carrier for East African Fruit Machine con-
cessions.

AMOS: Now . . . laddie . . . this is not the information I was led
to believe you had handed over freely and voluntarily back in
your cell this morning?

SINDI: No, sir.

AMOS: I'd like you to remind me, what facts you gave freely and
voluntarily, to these men?

SINDI: I had as sensible a conversation as I could with them, and
they duly informed me of their position. If I did not comply
freely and voluntarily, I would be 'finished off slowly' I think
are the exact words.

AMOS: Well . . . for your benefit I'll outline what this refers to.
They mean, dear lad, they take you to a quiet patch of
ground, and cut off your private pieces, these, along with
your tongue which by then you have also parted company
with are stuffed down your throat. Limb by limb you are
severed into portions. If you live long enough, you are
encouraged to eat portions of this broken–up anatomy.

SINDI: I see.

AMOS: Believe you me, it is a form of persuasion these men are
very accustomed to.

SINDI: Quite.

AMOS: Meanwhile, they did make it clear to you, just what
exactly they wanted you to tell them?

SINDI: Perfectly.

AMOS: And you have memorized all this?

SINDI: To the very best of my ability.

AMOS: Right then . . . shall we try again?

(*He pulls out a further length of notepaper. He draws the typewriter close to his chest and awkwardly fingers the keys.*)

Your full name is –

SINDI: Sindi Baru.

AMOS: Nationality?

SINDI: UK passport holder resident in Sudan.

AMOS: Your origin of birth?

SINDI: I was born in Staling Grove, Wolverhamptonshire.

AMOS: Wolverhampton.

SINDI: Wolverhamptonshire.

AMOS: No shire . . .

SINDI: I apologize.

AMOS: Present occupation?

SINDI: Spokesman and principal advocate, acting-chairman of the Society for Disenfranchised Asian Peoples –

AMOS: Communities.

SINDI: Society for Disenfranchised Asian Communities. If I may say so, sir – 'peoples' seems a much more democratic word than 'communities' with all its echoes of sectarian groupings.

AMOS: You could be right. Now – you are aware that this Society is banned in Uganda, and any propaganda affiliated hereto is also banned?

SINDI: I am.

AMOS: In addition – there is concern in Uganda about those who finance this Society. You are prepared freely and voluntarily to declare their names.

SINDI: It is a mixture of the CIA and various Zionist fronts from London and Paris, notably Marks and Spencers Ltd, Safeways and Pricerite stores, Tesco Trading Company and the Rothschild Banque Centrale, Avenue Marceau, Paris huitième.

AMOS: You immediately made contact once you arrived at Jinja, without having passed any normal Ugandan border posts, made contact with whom?

SINDI: An Englishman.

AMOS: His name?

SINDI: Angus Fraser.

AMOS: Where was this?

SINDI: Beneath the Chrysler-Africa billboard, Jinja south, Gadaphi Market Square.

AMOS: What was the point of this meeting?

SINDI: To ascertain just how much danger the remaining Ugandan Asians face if the President were to be assassinated by an Indian.

AMOS: By you, you mean.

SINDI: I discussed this point with my six interrogators from Command Post HQ, Kampala; and I persuaded them I do not know one end of a gun from the other. I was not prepared to go any further than this. I was not prepared to commit suicide. My name is now Sindi Baru, and my concern is for the safety of all Asians left in this country on behalf of this Society for Disenfranchised Asian Communities.

AMOS: Are you prepared to sign this document?

SINDI: It is on the understanding that I am not the fish the authorities are interested in – it is the Britisher, this man called Fraser.

AMOS: Correct.

SINDI: And furthermore, on the understanding that I will be immediately released, and allowed to leave the country.

AMOS: Almost correct.

SINDI: A hitch? Sir, do I hear?

AMOS: I am to give you clothes, and set you free once you have signed this document. There is no risk from anyone in this bungalow because I think you will discover the place is now empty but for you and me. Will you sign please?

(AMOS *pauses to watch* 'SINDI' *sign the document he pulls out from the typewriter. There is a duplicate.*)

SINDI: (*Glancing up*) . . . This . . . Sindi Baru . . . seems a remarkably silly person, if I may say so, someone who doesn't seem to know how to keep out of trouble?

(AMOS *collects both signed documents. He pulls out from a bag some loose clothing. Slacks and vest and sandals.* 'SINDI' *hastily slips in to them.*)

AMOS: My advice is . . . as quickly as you can get to the border. Wait until night. Walk in the coolness. You might make it to Jaluo in twenty hours. Avoid all lorries. Don't accept lifts. Trust no one.

SINDI: My papers please?

AMOS: Ahh . . . I think you will find, Mr Baru, it will be safer without any documentation whatsoever.

(AMOS *takes the passport, which is in the name of its rightful owner,* ISAID DEM ALA-MESSID JALLI, *and places it in a transparent zip-folder. He puts the folder in his inside pocket.* 'SINDI' *stares with dismay at* AMOS. *By* AMOS's *side the telephone commences to ring.* AMOS *reaches for it slowly.* 'SINDI' *hurriedly makes for the door.*)

(*A door to a cell. Bars.* 'ANGUS FRASER', *looking weak and tired is drawn towards the grill in the door. Single naked bulb.*)

VOICE: Dr Allnutt?

ANGUS: Is that you, Major?

VOICE: Never you mind who it is.

ANGUS: I would like the use of a telephone.

VOICE: Out of the question. I'm afraid there is only one public utility line working and you wouldn't like that one.

ANGUS: I want to see a representative from the French Consulate.

VOICE: That has already been put into action. Someone will come to you.

ANGUS: I'm hungry.

VOICE: When did you last eat?

ANGUS: I think perhaps two nights back. The time does strange things –

VOICE: Have you water?

ANGUS: I use the water kept in the disposal bucket. I put earth over my waste material.

VOICE: Perfectly sensible.

ANGUS: I didn't think I'd be grateful for an earth floor. How long will I be here?

VOICE: I do not know.

ANGUS: Is there any way that London or even a colleague can be informed?

VOICE: London is *au fait*.

ANGUS: Can they do anything?

VOICE: I'm afraid no.

ANGUS: I've . . . got a lady wife . . . and two boys . . . that I'd love . . . love to meet again.

VOICE: Steady . . . steady? . . .

ANGUS: Y . . . yes . . .

VOICE: Hang in there, what?

ANGUS: Not very apt recommendation this precise moment.

VOICE: Sorry about that . . . now – have you spoken to anyone?

ANGUS: No.

VOICE: No peculiar happenings?

ANGUS: Sometimes I hear firing . . . now and then the light bulb dies on me . . . I have for company what appears to be a five-legged rat who has two other chums, and when I wake up the lice tend to shelter in my nostrils although I have expressly forbidden this on account that any gathering of three persons or more shall be deemed a public meeting and carries a death penalty.

VOICE: Nobody has coerced you into signing anything?

ANGUS: Nothing.

VOICE: Right you are.

ANGUS: What will become of me?

VOICE: Touch wood old chap.

ANGUS: I tend to eat it rather than – present diet conditions.

VOICE: One final question, old boy – are you or have you ever been known as Angus Fraser or Dr Angus Fraser?

ANGUS: Never.

VOICE: Can you assure me of that? On oath?

ANGUS: There are only about three things worth making an oath upon – the Holy Bible, the Union Jack or one's mother. I don't possess the former, as for the latter two, they are both dead anyway. Would my life insurance do instead?

VOICE: That's it – keep up the chin.

ANGUS: (*Softly*) Help me . . . you bastard . . .

(*Silence.*)

. . . Major!

(*Lights change to the far corner where 'SINDI' [ISAID in reality] is walking across country at night. Occasionally truck lights flash past him. He blinks and walks on, bloody and dishevelled.*)

(*The lights lift on a vast bare area. More like a hangar but it is a disused passenger lounge at Entebbe. Filthy white walls. Litter and graffiti. Stars of David. Shaloms. Bullet holes everywhere. Broken glass upper panes. Steel doors barred with chains. Naked lamps swinging.*

AMOS enters, he does not see IDI immediately. Sound of gunfire. Bulbs flicker low. Beneath the windows lie the unmounted frames of a number of 106 mm nozzles. There are moments of complete light failure during this scene.)

AMOS: . . . Mr President, sir?

IDI: Present, Major.

AMOS: Ah . . . but there are no guards outside?

IDI: I leave these PLF fighters in the Command Post.

AMOS: But you have to have a bodyguard, sir – ?

IDI: No. Safer without.

AMOS: Sir – ?

IDI: I don't sleep well . . . men about men lying outside the door, men sitting on the window rails, I don't sleep so well. No privacy now.

AMOS: Price of fame and power, sir.

IDI: I am tired now.

AMOS: Yes sir, quite.

IDI: Better here . . . they all gone away.

AMOS: Absolutely and definitely . . . the mind needs respite . . . ease of mind . . . change the pace.

IDI: Yes, Major.

AMOS: V. refreshing, sir.

IDI: You done what I asked, Major?

AMOS: Sir!

IDI: You saw the Indian?

AMOS: Sir!

IDI: And that Britisher?

AMOS: Sir! The doctor.

IDI: I don't want Towilli's men torturing and brutalizing these men, I want to show them mercy, I want a public trial, here are these people with UK passports, here I have a UK passport. Brought to a fair trial and public punishment. A Ugandan Peoples' Tribunal.

AMOS: I spoke with the Britisher, sir.

IDI: What is his name?

AMOS: Name is . . . Angus Fraser, sir. No doubt about that.

IDI: The Indian?

AMOS: Name is Sindi Baru, sir. I have filed his complete confession with the State Research Bureau. He is a dead man.

IDI: Where is he?

AMOS: I put him back sir where he was first placed, the Makindye Military Prison.

IDI: The Britisher?

AMOS: I put him in the Makindye, sir.

IDI: I'd like to speak to them . . . tell them about their bad ways . . . but I feel sorry for them. Not their fault. Little people. Tools of the West. British tools. Oh Britain think they rule the waves the flag been rolled up long time gone now what the famous English weekly the *Spectator* say of me day of accession 30 January 1971 say – 'We cannot say we learn of the overthrow of Dr Milton Obote of Uganda with any great regret: if a choice is to be made between quiet military men and noisy civil dictators then we prefer in Africa at least the quiet military.' Say that, the English *Spectator*. Then say the weekly *New Statesman*, *New Statesman* 29 January 1971, say – 'So far as Britain is concerned Amin will undoubtedly be easier to deal with than the abrasive Obote!' Now . . . what they scheming – assassination they scheme. Bring that Indian in here to kill me. I had a dream. And I remembered his name. Forget it is Dada Amin they deal with they who invented me all those jokes clever English comics funny stories . . . I never ride the same jeep . . . never say where I go next . . . never tell them which wife I sleep with . . . who I eat with . . . run . . . run . . . keep on . . . an Olympic athlete Akii Bua would have won in Montreal if I had sent him . . . Now they think send me an Indian he has a chance, what, Major?

AMOS: Not a chance in the world, sir.

IDI: If he got to me, he could never get out of Uganda alive. I'd be a martyr.

AMOS: Absolutely, sir.

IDI: They know they cannot find a black boy dare try to kill me. Nobody not even my enemies would do that. They know what it look like just black Africa bunch of grape coons unable to keep peace between themselves always killing each other, funny niggers and wogs always behave like that.

AMOS: Not too many blacks would dare try, Mr President.

IDI: It is the perfect thing the British think, oh send some half-crazed Asian got a raw deal some time in Uganda, excuse enough get rid of him afterwards.

AMOS: Quite, sir. And I somehow don't think he would finish the job. All bunglers these bods, no army training behind, hit and miss.

IDI: What would you say, Major, if it was a white who tried assassinate Idi Amin?

AMOS: Not possible, sir.

IDI: Why not?

AMOS: No way out. Stands out a mile in this country. Certain death.

IDI: Impossible, Major?

AMOS: He'd have to lay plans mighty carefully. No border country could bail him out. He'd be entirely on his own, sir.

IDI: What he do it for, Major? The money?

AMOS: He couldn't escape.

IDI: You know who laughing if I die, Major? The right wing of the world laughing.

AMOS: Don't follow you, sir?

IDI: Little Asian get to me with a grenade or a revolver – Vorster laughing, Kissinger laughing, all these right-wing English papers laughing, Israel laughing, and France . . . But it would never be a white man. What do you say?

AMOS: Or perhaps he could lay a good false scent. Give him time to get out quite respectably.

(*The light bulbs are on the blink. Gunfire increases. Both men listen to it.*)

IDI: When I threw out those Asians, I paid Africa's debt in full. Why do you think Banda in Malawi has ordered all Asian shopkeepers out of the rural areas? The British put them here. They can take them away.

AMOS: Sir?

IDI: This is the old passenger embarkation room, Entebbe. I let those Jews stay here while I tried to barter for their lives. Kenya and CIA and New York Zionists attack, daren't see the OAU President make big success of the various top-level discussion, no good to see a black sergeant they want to topple make a hit with Israeli passengers I like Jews only want to see Dada Amin come down because they have a separate plan, nobody in entire history ever been assassinated in a vacuum, when I am gone look round your back garden and ask who profit and point your finger. You know who I had in here? Had meet me?

AMOS: Sir?

IDI: Oh all come here meet Amin . . . Kissinger arrive . . . big red carpet . . . Brezhnev arrive . . . Chou en-Lai . . . Whitlam . . . Gadaphi my friend . . . James Callaghan . . . West Germany man . . . French President before last . . . all come here . . . suddenly Uganda got the spotlight of the world . . . all black children look up see Big Daddy say yea I kill, yea my enemies will suffer, but this is a black African man saying too. He say children look up it will be blood at the tip of Africa, it will be Muslim and Marxist call-to-arms bring Namibia into arms of those black children what white man who can bomb Nagasaki can call a black leader a tyrant fear! (*The lights finally dim to nothing. Blackness. Gunfire in the distance.*)

IDI'S VOICE: Do you see, Major?

AMOS'S VOICE: Not a thing, sir.

(*In the darkness a square of light is lit. ALLNUTT is lying in a cramped earth dug-out no larger than a grave hole. He is bloodied and weak, but alive.*
The image blacks.)

IDI: Before the fall of Obote, people said I knew too much about Obote's ivory. And Obote collected ivory. And people said the British must have been involved in the plot against Obote. I never denied it.

(*The lights flicker back on. The firing fades away.*)

IDI: Talk to me, Major, less of this 'sir' and that 'sir', what you saying to me Major when you sleep at night?

AMOS: What would you like to hear me say, Mr President?

IDI: Talk about the past, Major. You remember the old past? We fought together against the Mau Mau. I was a corporal in the King's African Rifles. At Tuso we killed them, at Kairo, at Kinyono, and Kangema we killed them down. Then in Karamoja we degooded the Pokot tribe, and one whole Turkana village we provided them with a proper funeral, wasn't that so, Major?

AMOS: Sir?

IDI: It was the past wasn't it? It was there then. And I was still the sergeant. Though I was the heavyweight champion of Uganda. I think . . . I still am the heavyweight champion of Uganda. As a sergeant I'd go up to the barrack Commander, Major Iain Grahame, I'd say look at these new officers you have made, sir! Lieutenant Okahura, Lieutenant Ndalebo, Lieutenant Oyite, all drunk sir, dogs lying kicking their legs up all *pombe* drunk, sir! But not me, sir, I am a Muslim.

AMOS: Absolutely.

IDI: Talk to me about the old King's African Rifles . . . ?

AMOS: Ah . . . ehr . . . Mr President remembers those happy days recruiting in Karamoja in '62. When you asked a Suk recruit to kill a snake to test his accuracy he said, oh no, he said, the soul of the dead Suk always returned into a snake. So Mr President spends the next two weeks shooting every damn snake he can see in the bush to try break the silly superstition.

IDI: (*Smiling warmly*) Never broke it for good.

AMOS: Sir remembers the day whites opened up the officers' messroom to all African officers and senior men and when I walked in with you and you ordered a beer that Asian barman was so scared of serving you I had to take him by the throat and shake him like a rattlesnake tell him it's all right you silly bleeder the sergeant can be served a beer!

IDI: He ran out the door like a wildebeest!

AMOS: There was old Colonel Tom 'Diddles' Parker . . . Old Parksy . . . Fossbender with the white eyebrows.

IDI: Captain Henry Fossbender.

AMOS: Larry Merridew.

IDI: Lieutenant the medic always filled his syringes with water always did the trick the men never came back with another complaint!

AMOS: Marcos Rodd.

IDI: Old Mauritio . . . what he do Mauritio now, he went to Fort Portal –

AMOS: They say he bought out the entire boot quota from the British for a thousand shillings, he set up shop with more boots than we could –

IDI: I tell you he had more boots than we got Ugandans in the whole of Uganda!

AMOS: That's right, sir! Jolly funny story.

IDI: You went to Sandhurst, Amos?

AMOS: Sir.

IDI: High-class English school?

AMOS: Haileybury, sir.

IDI: And you went abroad?

AMOS: Gibraltar, Hong Kong, Malaya, NATO serving in Turkey, relief-force volunteers in the Trucial States . . . everywhere, sir.

IDI: Yes. And you met the Queen?

AMOS: I had the honour of an introduction once from the one-time governor of Kenya, Sir Evelyn Baring.

IDI: But you never took a wife?

AMOS: I . . . keep out of trouble, sir.

IDI: What do you stay for here in Uganda?

AMOS: If sir recalls, I am now a Ugandan citizen. Long time since have I given up my home passport. There is no leaving . . .

IDI: But, what do you stay for, Amos?

AMOS: Well, sir, if you had seen it the way I have. Up country, the Rift Valley, Murchison National Park, the Karamajong

Hills . . . the Owen Falls hydro-electric scheme . . . I have
stood on the shores of Lake Victoria and watched the night
come down, I've watched so many purple herons, fifteen
thousand or more of them, as if in separate squadrons, take
an hour to flight off, to clear in the dead sun . . . you'd
understand . . . this land is the pearl, sir.

IDI: You are the officer and the gentleman I trust.

AMOS: Sir!

IDI: All those things I say about the West don't count . . . Amos
. . . remember it was me I was the butt sergeant.

AMOS: And I was, *pro tem.*, your Commanding Officer.

IDI: (*Standing*) Firing ceased now. I think my wives ceased their
quarrelling.

AMOS: Sir!

(AMOS *walks away from the figure in the corner of the passenger
lounge.*)

IDI: I go, now.

AMOS: Sir.

IDI: I go home.

(AMOS *pauses by an unlocked door. He looks back. Takes a step
back towards* IDI.)

AMOS: There was one more thing . . . sir . . . with respect.

(IDI *glances up.*)

IDI: I must go.

AMOS: Mr President . . .

(AMOS *slowly reaches for something in his pocket.
He draws the gun and fires.*)

Mr President, I have a message for you from a number of old
friends of yours outside Uganda – It is a message from the
following – Brigadier Muhammed Hussein, and Colonels
M. Arach, A. Langoya, Akwango, Ojok, Abwala, Ayumi,
Ekirring, P. Obol, O. Ogwal; the soldiers and friends of
Lugbara, the men and women of Mbarara, former Prime
Minister of Uganda, Kiwanua; Vice-Chancellor of Makerere
University, Kalimuzo; Governor of the Bank of Uganda,
Mubiru; the Chief-Justice of Uganda, Benedicto Kiwanuka
and Archbishop Luwum.

(AMOS *puts the revolver away. He takes the waterproof zip-folder from his pocket. He takes out Isaid's passport and tosses it on the ground beside the body.*

AMOS *pauses. In his mind he hears a very faint echo of a military command. As of a parade ground command to muster.*

AMOS *stares steadily at us. His eyeline is strangely fixed above our heads now. Gradually, there comes the sound of a military band. It is an echo in* AMOS's *mind of a flag being lowered and a ceremonial strike up.*

As the music fades away, AMOS *turns and walks off.*

Comes a different sound, far away, that of the British marching out of Uganda.

Lights change.)

ACT THREE
Incidental Flashback

Beneath the Chrysler-Africa billboard, Jinja south, Gadaphi Market Square. The neon blinks above the heads of the crowds. Two strangers pass by. They are ISAID DEM ALA-MESSID JALLI *and* GREVILLE WILLIAM ALLNUTT. ISAID *sees* GREVILLE *look for a match for his cigarette.* GREVILLE *has a newspaper sticking out of his pocket.*

GREVILLE: Ah . . . excuse me, have you a light?

ISAID: Here . . .

GREVILLE: Thank you . . .

ISAID: Is that a newspaper you have?

GREVILLE: What?

ISAID: The *Voice of Uganda* you have there?

GREVILLE: Matter of fact it's the *Times of Zambia.*

ISAID: Today's *Times?*

GREVILLE: Oh no.

ISAID: Yesterday's?

GREVILLE: Four days old.

ISAID: I see . . . There has been no radio all day, I thought perhaps. It has been such a terrible day for me.

GREVILLE: Sorry to hear that.

ISAID: But thank you. There was nothing much of particular importance in it?

GREVILLE: No, nothing at all.

ISAID: No news, sir?

GREVILLE: Do keep it. Here.

> (GREVILLE *gives the paper to* ISAID. *They nod and go their ways amongst the crowd.*
> *Traffic and sellers and the billboard flicker.*
> *The noises diminish. Urban shadows retreat. A dust haze settles.*

LEE HARVEY OSWALD

a far mean streak of indepence brought on by
negleck

PRESIDENT'S COMMISSION ON THE ASSASSINATION OF PRESIDENT KENNEDY

Chief Justice Earl Warren, Chairman
Senator Richard B. Russell
Senator John Sherman Cooper
Representative Hale Boggs
Representative Gerald R. Ford
Mr Allen W. Dulles
Mr John J. McCloy
J. Lee Rankin, General Counsel

Established by President Lyndon B. Johnson
29 November 1963

Report of the President's Commission on the Assassination of President John F. Kennedy (Warren Commission Report). 888 pages. Published 27 September 1964

Hearings Before the President's Commission on the Assassination of President Kennedy
26 volumes – Testimony and Exhibits. Published 23 November 1964

'Lee Harvey Oswald was born in Oct 1939 in New Orleans, La. The son of a Insuraen Salesmen whose early death left a far mean streak of indepence brought on by negleck . . .'

'I wonder what would happen if somebody was to stand up and say he was utterly opposed not only to the governments, but to the people, to the entire land and complete foundations of his socially . . .'

'In the event of war, I would kill any american who put a uniform on in defence of the american government – any american.'

Two extracts, in the original spelling, from Oswald's Historic Diary, and an extract from a letter from Russia to his brother Robert

CHARACTERS

SPEAKER
COMMISSION
MARINA, *Lee's wife*
MARGUERITE, *his mother*
LEE

Lee Harvey Oswald: a far mean streak of indepence brought on by negleck was first performed at the Hampstead Theatre, 22 November 1966.

SPEAKER COMMISSION	Ronan O'Casey
MARINA	Sarah Miles
MARGUERITE	Bessie Love
LEE	Alan Dobie
DIRECTOR	Peter Coe
DESIGNER	Michael Knight

PROLOGUE

The stage is lit. On the stage hangs a white screen. There is a single stool.
The backcloth is dark. The SPEAKER *walks out front. He sits. He*
talks . . .

SPEAKER: . . . 1939, in New Orleans, Lee Harvey Oswald was
born.[1] His father Robert had died two months before. Lee
had an older half-brother,[2] by a previous marriage – his own
brother was five years his senior.[3] Lee Oswald had a dog, he
collected stamps and played chess and truant. Given pro-
bation for his frequent truancy, a social worker's report
suggested Oswald was a withdrawn and maladjusted boy.
The relationship between mother and son was tense. Aged
sixteen he wrote to the Socialist Party of America – 'I am a
Marxist.' Aged sixteen he failed to join the Marine Corps
Reserve; his mother would not let him falsify his age. He had
to wait for his seventeenth birthday. For a whole year he
lived for the day he could join up. In the Marine Corps he
learnt radar and studied Russian. He still kept few friends.
Then Oswald applied for a discharge – apparently his mother
could not support herself at home. He received an 'undesir-
able discharge'.[4] He had also made an application to a school
for philosophy and science in Switzerland.[5] Home again
briefly, he gave his mother a hundred dollars; six days later he

1. 18 October 1939.
2. John Edward Pic.
3. Robert Oswald.
4. 13 September 1960.
5. Albert Schweitzer College, Churwalden, Switzerland. 19 March 1959.

was on a ship in New Orleans.[1] He wrote to his mother –
'Well I have booked passage on a ship to Europe, I would of
had to sooner or later and I think its best I go now.' Le Havre,
London, Helsinki, Moscow, and to Minsk, where he worked
in a factory. Lee applied for Russian citizenship. He tried
to renounce his passport. He fell in love with a girl,[2] she
would not wed him, he married another. She was Marina
Prusakova. She was nineteen. A baby daughter, June Lee,
was born. They both decided to return to the States. The
American Embassy loaned them cash,[3] and via Moscow,
Minsk, Brest their train brought them to Holland. Across the
Atlantic to New York,[4] from there they flew to Texas.[5] Lee
Oswald was twenty-one.

These facts seem dull beside the tragic actions which
followed. But the early years must be paraphrased – the sum
of a man is in his waking.

The Oswalds stayed with friends. They moved from one
room to one cold-water apartment to one room again and
again. Lee Oswald took numerous jobs, he never ceased
searching for congenial employment. The pattern of his life
was the same – erratic, uncertain, he was unable to cope with
the America to which he had come back.

He left for New Orleans[6] where he was involved in a
strange enterprise. He printed leaflets which read HANDS
OFF CUBA. He described himself as a branch of the Fair Play
for Cuba Committee. He also befriended various anti-Castro
refugees who were openly plotting against the Cuban
regime.[7] One day his friends found him distributing his
leaflets. They attacked him. They were arrested, and Oswald
was jailed for a night. Why?

Later Lee and Marina separated. Marina lived with a

1. 20 September 1960. S.S. Marion Lykes.
2. Ella German.
3. $435 71c.
4. S.S. Maarsdam at Hoboken New Jersey. 13 June 1962.
5. 14 June 1962.
6. 5 August 1963.
7. Carlos Bringuier. Rolando Paez. Celso Hernandez. Miguel Cruz.

friend.[1] Lee left for Mexico City.[2] He applied at the Cuban Embassy for an 'in-transit' visa to permit him to travel to Russia via Cuba.[3] He was advised to apply at the Russian Embassy, which he did. He was told it would take time to arrange it. He seemed upset and impatient. He stayed for a week, then left for Texas.[4]

On October 18, he applied at the Book Depository building, and the Superintendent Roy S. Truly hired him in a temporary capacity.

One month later, President John F. Kennedy was assassinated by gunfire in Dallas.

These are the barest facts of Oswald's life with the least embellishments that can be contrived.

(*The lights change. The white screen is lit. The* SPEAKER *uses a stick to mark areas.*)

. . . on Friday morning, 22 November 1963, the President arrived with his party at Love Field, Dallas.[5] The motorcade drove through downtown Dallas towards the Trade Mart for a luncheon speech.

(*Film of the motorcade commences.*)

. . . This is Dealey Plaza. The motorcade turns left on Houston Street into Elm Street.

(*A still of the scene is shown.*)

. . . This is the Book Depository store. Here is the sixth-floor window . . . The overpass . . . the car-port . . . the trees in front of the Depository building . . . the trees in front of the car-port . . . and the slightly rising knoll – here. The bullets began to hit the car here.

[6](*A still from the film of the shooting. The car is driving along slowly; the President smiles and waves. Before the first bullet hits, the frame freezes.*)

1. Mrs Ruth Paine. Irving, Dallas.
2. 25 September 1963.
3. Warren Commission Report, pp. 280–82.
4. 3 October 1963.
5. 11.40 a.m. Friday 22 November 1963.
6. The sequence from this point to the end of the first paragraph on p. 151 is interchangeable. It can be placed after Marina's line on p. 220, 'Yes I am convinced.'

More than four hundred people were in or around Dealey Plaza when the assassination occurred. Two hundred and sixty-six witnesses to the crime are known. Of these, ninety were asked from where did the shots come. Fifty-eight witnesses said that the shots came from the direction of the grassy knoll, to the right fore-front of the car; the other thirty-two witnesses said otherwise.

(*The film moves again. The bullets hit President Kennedy, Governor Connally, and the car. The car gathers speed and pulls away. The film shows the general chaos of Dealey Plaza. People running, standing, or lying on the ground.*)

Abraham Zapruder, with an 8-millimetre camera, filmed the actual shooting from the bank leading up to the grass knoll.

(*Still of scene.*)

Zapruder's film runs at 18.3 frames per second. The earliest possible moment a bullet from the Book Depository store could have hit the car with clear view of the car is after frame 210, because up to that frame an oak tree obscures the view of the car from the sixth floor window.

(*Still of first shot.*)

The President was first hit at frame 225.[1] The Governor sitting in front of him was hit by a subsequent bullet. You see the President being hit first . . .

(*Still.*)

Then you see Connally turn to his right to look behind him. He cannot see the President, so he turns to his left.

(*Still.*)

Then he too is hit.

(*Still.*)

The Zapruder film shows that Connally was hit between frames 230 and 240. Now, it is universally acknowledged that any bullet fired from the 6.5 millimetre Mannlicher-Carcano rifle which it is claimed Oswald fired that day, needs a minimum of 2.3 seconds between firing. These are the Warren Commission's findings using expert riflemen. But

1. *Hearings*, XVIII, p. 26.

2.3 seconds between bullets amounts to 42.09 frames on Zapruder's 8 millimetre film. What this amounts to is – no bullet from that gun, whether the first strike was fired at 210 frames or 225 frames – no bullet from that gun could hit again by frame 240 – when the Governor was struck. Governor Connally testified to the Commission that he heard the first bullet crack. By then it had reached its target. He turned to the right, then to the left, and then he was hit. He testified he could not hear the second bullet fire. Which is not surprising. The Governor and his wife testified to the best of their knowledge that Connally was hit by a second bullet. The Warren Commission maintain that one bullet and one bullet only hit the President and then simultaneously crashed into the Governor's ribs, splintered his right wrist and lodged in his left thigh. In all there were five bullet wounds, two on the President, three on the Governor; some kind of fragment starred the car's windshield, and a bullet two grains lighter than its normal weight was found inside the car; there was a bullet in the Governor's thigh, and one bullet, the first, had ranged down inside the President's body. A further bullet was found on Governor Connally's stretcher at the hospital. This might appear to sound as if more than three bullets were fired. But this is a point the Warren Commission have not denied. It is possible – they suggest that one bullet missed altogether. But the Zapruder film which *Life* magazine owns exclusive rights to, does make it all too clear that the first two bullets could not have been fired from that one gun, the 6.5 millimetre Mannlicher-Carcano. That gun cannot fire again in 1.3 seconds; the bolt action won't lift the bullet for the trigger finger to align and fire in that time. That Mannlicher-Carcano rifle was twenty-five years old; Oswald paid $10 for it by mail-order. The ammunition for it was no less old . . .

A forty-five-year-old steamfitter, Howard Brennan, was the only witness to identify Lee Harvey Oswald as the man who fired the rifle. He was across the street from the Book Depository. He was a hundred feet from the building wall, and about 120 feet from the south-east corner window of the sixth floor. Brennan swore the man was standing up and firing. To fire from that window, sixty feet up on the sixth floor, one must either kneel or lie; the lattice window slides up only at the bottom. If Oswald fired that gun from that window, which was sixty feet from the ground, he was hitting a slow-moving target, with a sight attachment, at 260 feet with a twenty-seven degree angle. For this feat the Warren Commission allows him seven seconds.

After the shooting at 12.33 that morning, Oswald, it is claimed, was stopped by an officer[1] for a moment, in the canteen inside the building; the officer was told he was an employee, the officer ran on. Oswald left the building, walked seven blocks on Elm Street where the firing had been, took a bus which turned back towards Elm Street, got out of the bus, walked several more blocks, took a taxi ride, walked more blocks to his room, where he stayed a couple of minutes to change, hurriedly left, waited at a bus stop, then walked almost a mile to Patton Avenue. There, he himself approached a police car, leant inside, stepped away and turned and gunned down the Officer J. D. Tippit who suddenly leapt out of the car. All in forty-three minutes. Tippit was killed at about 1.15.

(*The film of Oswald's brief press conference comes on the screen. The hurried voices, the shoutings.*)

If Oswald had been tried in a court of law, he would have been presented with the evidence of his palm-print on a gun he undoubtedly owned; he certainly would have been charged with the murder of Officer Tippit; and the witness to him shooting from the Book Depository building, and the other witness to him killing Tippit . . . but his wife Marina could never have testified against him as she has done. Howard Brennan, who claims he saw Oswald fire from a sixth-floor window at the motorcade, and Helen Markham,[2] who says she saw Oswald shoot down Tippit – their reliability is in question; what they might say in court is not absolutely watertight. There are great grave masses of mys-

---

1. Marrion L. Baker.
2. *Vide* testimonies of Benavides, Clemons, Scoggins, Higgins, Davis, Calloway and Reynolds.

tery the Warren Commission have not cleared up. Lee Harvey Oswald spent forty-eight hours in the Dallas police station until at 11.21 a.m. he was gunned down by Jack Ruby with a single shot. Oswald was being transferred to the County jail.

(*The film of Ruby approaching Oswald in the basement of the station; Ruby firing his gun. Oswald collapsing.*)

There are strange stories. There is circumstantial evidence about Ruby himself, and his involvement in Cuban activities.[1] Nobody can really explain why, fifteen minutes after the shooting of the President, such an intense witch-hunt of Oswald took place.[2] Nor can anyone, least of all the Warren Commission, explain why John F. Kennedy was gunned down that day. The more years that pass, the more rumours. The speculation becomes myth, and the myth presents a parody of reality.

What is irrefutable is the speed with which the first two bullets were fired.[3]

What is indelible in our minds is that the President's head received a fatal strike from the last bullet – which was either the third or the fourth shot.

Three doctors, on that fatal Friday, announced at their press conference that the wound on the President's neck had the appearance of an entry wound.[4]

Later, after the FBI pressed them to reconsider their verdict, the doctors at Parkland Memorial Hospital reversed their judgement.

It is not possible to know who has seen the photographs of the wounds or the X-ray pictures.

If Lee Harvey Oswald did it, he could not have done it

1. *Hearings*, XIV, pp. 330–64. Testimony of Nancy Perrin Rich.
2. A description of the suspect in the assassination matching Oswald's description, was broadcast by the Dallas police just before 12.45 p.m. on 22 November.
3. Warren Commission Report, p. 106.
4. Dr Malcolm Perry, Dr Kemp Clark. *New York Times*, 23 November 1963. Dr Charles Carrico. *Hearings*, XVIII, p. 2.

alone. If he did not, he must be the hit[1] of the century. If he was involved, and somehow double-crossed, alive today must be persons with the guilt of silence.

1. Stool pigeon.

ACT ONE

The stage is dark. Three figures stand in the foreground. A voice speaks from the audience. MARINA *is lit.*

COMMISSION: Mrs Oswald you be at your ease, and the interpreter will tell you what I ask and you take your time about your answers. Will you state your name please?

MARINA: Marina, my name is Marina Nikolaevna Oswald. My maiden name was Prusakova.

COMMISSION: Where do you live Mrs Oswald?

MARINA: At the present time I live in Dallas . . .

COMMISSION: Mrs Oswald do you have a family?

MARINA: I have two children, two girls, June will be two years old in February, and Rachel is three months old.

COMMISSION: Are you the widow of the late Lee Harvey Oswald?

MARINA: Yes . . .

COMMISSION: Do you recall the date that you arrived in the United States with your husband Lee Harvey Oswald?

MARINA: On the 13th of June 1962. I am not quite certain as to the year – 61 or 62 I think 62.

COMMISSION: How did you come to this country?

MARINA: From Moscow via Poland, Germany and Holland, we came to Amsterdam by train. And from Amsterdam to New York by ship, and New York to Dallas by air.

COMMISSION: Do you recall the name of the ship on which you came?

MARINA: I think it was the S.S. Rotterdam but I am not sure.

COMMISSION: What time of the day did you arrive in New York?

MARINA: It was about noon – or 1 p.m. – thereabouts. It is hard to remember the exact time.

COMMISSION: How long did you stay in New York at that time?

MARINA: We stayed that evening and the next twenty-four hours in a hotel in New York. And then we left the following day by air.

COMMISSION: Did you know whether or not you or your husband received any financial assistance for the trip to Texas? At that time?

MARINA: I don't know exactly where Lee got the money, but he said that his brother Robert had given him the money. But the money for the trip from the Soviet Union to New York was given to us by the American Embassy in Moscow.

COMMISSION: Do you recall what time of the day you left on the flight to Texas?

MARINA: I think that by about 5 p.m. we were already in Texas.

COMMISSION: Did you go to Dallas or Fort Worth at that time?

MARINA: In Dallas we were met by the brother, Robert, he lived in Fort Worth, and he took us from Dallas to Forth Worth and we stopped at the house.

COMMISSION: Who else stayed at Robert's house at that time besides your family?

MARINA: His family and no one else.

COMMISSION: What did his family consist of at that time?

MARINA: He and his wife, and two children a boy and a girl.

COMMISSION: How long did you stay at Robert's?

MARINA: About one to one and a half months, perhaps longer, but no longer than two months.

COMMISSION: Were your relations and your husband's with Robert pleasant at that time?

MARINA: Yes they were very good. His brother's relationship to us was very good.

COMMISSION: Would you briefly describe what you did during that time when you were at Robert's?

MARINA: The first time we got there we were, of course, resting for about a week, and I was busy, of course, with my little girl who was then very little. And in my free time, of course, I helped in the household.

COMMISSION: Did your husband do anything around the house or did he seek work right away?

MARINA: For about a week he was merely talking and took a trip to the library. That is it.

COMMISSION: Then did he seek work in Fort Worth?

MARINA: Yes.

COMMISSION: And when did he find his first job there?

MARINA: While we were with Robert. It seems it was at the end of the second month that Lee found work. But at this time I don't remember the date exactly, but his mother who lived in Fort Worth at that time rented a room and she proposed that we spend some time with her, that we live with her for some time.

COMMISSION: Did you discuss with your husband this proposal of your mother-in-law to have you live with her?

MARINA: Well, she made the proposal to my husband, not to me. Of course I found out about it.

COMMISSION: Did you and he have any discussion about it after you found out about it?

MARINA: Yes, of course.

COMMISSION: You recall that discussion?

MARINA: No. I only remember the fact.

COMMISSION: Did he find work after you left Robert's then?

MARINA: Yes.

COMMISSION: You did move to be with your mother-in-law, lived with her for a time?

MARINA: Yes about three weeks. And then after three weeks Lee did not want to live with her any more and he rented an apartment.

COMMISSION: Did you know the reason why he did not want to live there any more?

MARINA: It seemed peculiar to me and didn't want to believe it but he did not love his mother, she was not quite a normal woman. Now I know this for sure.

COMMISSION: Did he tell you that at the time?

MARINA: He talked about it but since he . . .

(She steps away into the darkness.

The light comes up. MARGUERITE *and* LEE *are talking.* MARINA *joins them quite naturally as if she has been in the room with them all the time.* LEE *takes a chair and sits down as if he is tired*.)

MARGUERITE: . . . I didn't even ask when you went out I didn't even ask – did I ask? If you want to go right down along there and try I'd say baby you try my honey – who would step up and argue when a clean-limbed young intelligent American steps off of this boat and all from Moscow – and all he has he can get is thirty dollars a week – I know that's criminal – but I don't stand up and say you deserve better boy – I leave that unto you –

MARINA: What is she saying?

MARGUERITE: Tried mind you – well I did – and that long trip out to Washington knowing all on you all alone in that foreign country – I'd still call it foreign you married or none to Marina – I went up to complain that they weren't hurrying enough that their fingers weren't none out not one bit – that – that I said to them.

MARINA: Oh Lee – will you please tell me –

MARGUERITE: Time to bring you back on home and forget. Won't they let a young man forget?

MARINA: Lee – you won't hear me – now what is she telling you to – do – is she angry with me? What does she shout Lee?

MARGUERITE: Even if I found you a room – it's only a room – and I take it from the man – it has loving all in it – for you to do with you what you want –

LEE: Mamma says I owe –

MARINA: Go on –

MARGUERITE: Time passes on like the Bible and some say the love that one has had passes well I am old and I am young because I see in me the time stays – now –

LEE: She helped us from Russia she says –

MARINA: We can pay it back –

LEE: Sacrificed jobs and all she say.

MARINA: But speak to her.

LEE: I cannot.

MARINA: Isn't all this hers isn't it true?

LEE: Not true enough – don't ask me what's not true . . .

MARGUERITE: And practise your Russian – well practise it – but

I'm practising the love of a mother not practising practising –
so I expect –

LEE: Not nothing do you!

MARGUERITE: Don't shout me down –

LEE: I'm sorry –

MARINA: Are you shouting at Mamma, Lee?

LEE: (*At the top of his voice*) No! Not! Shouting!

MARGUERITE: When I talk with you you won't talk – when you
talk to Marina I can't understand – and you won't say what
you say – what is it Lee? I should die? And my broken heart
and I?

LEE: Never could Mamma.

MARGUERITE: Yes . . . there was a time?

LEE: Not loving Mamma.

MARGUERITE: Plenty of nights lie in my arms and you say
whatever you thought the world outside had done – and
there was peace I gave you peace.

LEE: I shared a bed with you Mamma until I was ten – I never
could cry – could I ever say could I what I said – most times I
disliked the schools and places because I never could say what
it was so how could I say to you in bed – I never learnt to cry
remember that? Not me. So what tears Mamma?

MARGUERITE: I saw tears . . .

LEE: No Mamma . . . we're going on.

MARGUERITE: Isn't it cheap enough – is it a dollar overmuch?

LEE: Mamma we don't live together – I have Marina –

MARGUERITE: You need me.

LEE: I have Marina.

(*The stage darkens again.* MARGUERITE'*s voice can be heard. She
walks to the front of the stage. But it is still dark.*)

MARGUERITE'S VOICE: . . . and also stating that my son wishes
to return back to the United States – just eight weeks after my
trip to Washington.

(*We can see her clearly now. A spot lights her body. She is
addressing the audience.*)

MARGUERITE: Now, you want to know why I think my son is an
agent. And I have been telling you all along. Here is a very
important thing why my son was an agent. On 22 March I

receive a letter of his address and stating that my son wishes to return back to the United States. You have that sir?

COMMISSION: Yes.

MARGUERITE: On 30 April 1961, he marries a Russian girl – approximately five weeks later. Now why does a man who wants to come back to the United States, five weeks later – here is the proof: 30 April 1961, is the wedding date – marry a Russian girl? Because I say – and I may be wrong – the US Embassy has ordered him to marry this Russian girl. And a few weeks later, 16 May 1961, he is coming home with the Russian girl. And as we know, he does get out of the Soviet Union with the Russian girl, with money loaned to him by the US Embassy. I may be wrong gentlemen, but two and two in my book makes four.

COMMISSION: Mrs Oswald – you saw your daughter-in-law and your son living together with you, didn't you, for some time?

MARGUERITE: Yes, they lived with me one month.

COMMISSION: Did you think they were in love with each other?

MARGUERITE: Yes they were definitely in love with each other. Yes I think they were in love with each other.

COMMISSION: What about books? Did he read books much while he was living with you?

MARGUERITE: Yes he read continuously. He went immediately to the library upon coming to the United States. He read continuously. All kinds of books.

COMMISSION: Now was there any time that Marina said anything to you to lead you to believe that she thought your son, Lee, married her because he was an agent?

MARGUERITE: No Sir no Sir not at any time at all.

COMMISSION: You think she loved him?

MARGUERITE: I believe that Marina loved him in a way. But I believe that Marina wanted to come to America. I believe that Lee had talked American to her, and she wanted to come to America. Maybe she loved him. I am sure she did anyway. She said that she did.

COMMISSION: I am not clear about this being ordered to marry her. You don't mean that your son didn't love her?

MARGUERITE: Well I could mean that – if he is an agent, and he has a girlfriend, and it is to the benefit of the country that he marry this girlfriend, and the Embassy helped him to get this Russian girl out of Russia, let's face it, whether he loved her or not, he would take her to America, if that would give him contact with Russians, yes, sir.

COMMISSION: Is that what you mean?

MARGUERITE: I would say that.

COMMISSION: How did you get along when you were there together with Marina and your son?

MARGUERITE: Well that was a very happy month. Marina was very happy. She had the best home I believe that she had ever had . . .

(*The stage lights up again. She walks back to* LEE *who is where he was in the earlier scene* MARINA *described.*)

. . . I didn't even ask you when you went out I didn't even ask – did I ask? If you want to go right down along there and try I'd say baby you try my honey.

MARINA: Lee please –

LEE: I can't get no job – I got to get work –

MARGUERITE: But that's why you go down at the library – and you learn –

LEE: You don't see – I'm married – not in a cot now –

MARGUERITE: Are you married? I mean you suddenly got yourself a wife and a child – but do I come in there – I mean where do I come in there – I mean where do I come in – I'm saying nobody forgets a mother –

LEE: I know that Mamma – but Marina must eat – so must I – and June too – I ain't living off you none –

MARGUERITE: Did you ever?

LEE: I tried hard – you ask Robert – he knows – we all know we never wanted to live off of you – now did we?

MARGUERITE: Time was –

LEE: That's sentiment Mamma. Time is. I learn something a little bit everywhere – there's more'n in this world to hate than there is to like –

MARINA: Lee – say to me what she says?

LEE: I say nobody's happy –

MARINA: Lee say to me you love me?

LEE: Oh yes.

MARGUERITE: God knows I've been good.

LEE: What does that mean?

MARGUERITE: You and I have loved – and Robert too – in New York remember?

LEE: But I ran away far enough –

MARGUERITE: From the government from the system – oh I know there's a system you hate –

LEE: It's just – I mean just possibly it is the thing I hate which you can't really hate –

MARGUERITE: You love me Lee –

LEE: That's what I hate Mamma.

MARGUERITE: No . . .

LEE: And we go on talking love and fellow man – and there's Washington and Lincoln who are dead, and Marx is dead, and we feebly talk on love – what does it – it makes the world go on round?

MARGUERITE: I'm bitterly upset –

LEE: No.

MARGUERITE: You force me out – now if I go out and get something nice even if it's for Marina here who doesn't hear me when I say –

LEE: You can't afford it –

MARGUERITE: Afford love?

LEE: I didn't say that –

MARGUERITE: Nevertheless . . .

(*She puts on a coat and walks away.* LEE *tries to follow her.*)

LEE: It's not gifts – and – and – it's not love –

MARGUERITE: You say right on – one more word – you forcing me on like this.

(LEE *stands haplessly. He watches her go.*)

MARINA: Lee please?

LEE: She feels guilt –

MARINA: I sat here and listened – and you both don't speak to me –

LEE: Darling – she never does anything – Mamma likes to talk because she feels all the time – and she has never done life – she feels it – I do it –

MARINA: I'd like –

LEE: I feel I'm losing my hair that it's falling out – that's a feeling – but I'm not standing up in Congress and say all that for it – you stand up and say world you say world and democracies – and wrongs – oh there are wrongs.

MARINA: I'd like the television box on please Lee –

LEE: And when you got democracies you have here votes which none use properly – you say what? What?

MARINA: Gregory Peck.

LEE: Honey I'm not counting with you –

MARINA: Mamma said there was Gregory Peck this afternoon – could I see him. We have him – he was showing in Minsk remember –

LEE: No you cannot.

MARINA: I need to learn –

LEE: There's my way. Don't need no commercial slick hogwash – about Hollywood? Oh come on now . . . !

MARINA: June is sleeping.

LEE: Let me tell you – Gregory Peck will as certain as the red sun make June holler now – and all night.

MARINA: Then I do nothing.

LEE: No you don't.

MARINA: There'll be no washed dishes and Mamma will call you out for that –

LEE: You sit down.

MARINA: I'm sitting down –

LEE: Now I'll sit here –

MARINA: Did you love that other girl in Minsk – the girl in your diary – love her more than –

LEE: I won't discuss love!

MARINA: Ordinary people need to –

LEE: I am not ordinary. I'll discuss books, politics and great men – because that's all we ever learn from – I'm giving you learning now – will you watch?

MARINA: No. I want Gregory Peck.

LEE: What is that?

MARINA: I'm not blind.

LEE: I'm holding it up – now what is that?

MARINA: Ormin.

LEE: What do you mean 'ormin'.

MARINA: Orm.

LEE: *This* is my orm – I mean 'arm', not orm nothing Marina – but I'm holding up this –
> (MARINA *'climbs' up his arm and kisses the fingers on his hand.*)
Say – hand?

MARINA: Haarrnd.

LEE: It's hand.

MARINA: Aarnd.

LEE: Marina – what would you say if I said my harrnd ais oown moi ormin?

MARINA: That's very good – ten out of ten!
> (*She laughs.* LEE *sits humoured but saddened, shakes his head.*)

LEE: In English – what do you write on – or – no – what do you read?

MARINA: Book?

LEE: Very good. And when I nod my head what do we mean –

MARINA: Yes Mamma.

LEE: No Mamma!

MARINA: No Mamma.

LEE: When I go up and down like this?

MARINA: Yes Mamma.

> (*The lights dim a little.* LEE *and* MARINA *continue talking. Their voices fade.*
>
> *A spot picks out* MARGUERITE *who faces the audience. She holds in her hand a child's highchair. The rest of the stage is dark.*)

MARGUERITE: And of course Marina and Lee spoke Russian all the time even in front of me. And you asked me about this time – it was a happy time. They would sit at the table, they were playing a game, and I said to Lee what is it you are doing? Because they were always talking in Russian. Mother – we are playing a game which is similar to American tic-tac-toe. And they also taught each other. They had books. They are both children – very intelligent and studious. Lee was teaching Marina English, and Marina was teaching him some things that he wanted to know about Russia, in my home.

(*The lights come up. She walks around the stage. She comes in again where she left them both before.*
LEE *is still teaching* MARINA.)

LEE: There is in this room – what is there Marina?

MARINA: (*Points out objects slowly*) . . . table . . . book . . . chair
. . . Lee . . . television box.
(MARGUERITE *bustles in.*)
. . . Mamma!

MARGUERITE: Give that to her – tell her Lee –

LEE: No I refuse to.

MARGUERITE: Then I'll do it myself.

LEE: You do these things because you're guilty or something –
(MARGUERITE *hands the highchair to* MARINA *gently.* MARINA *is confused.*)

MARINA: How do I say thank you Lee? Is it for me Lee?

LEE: You say no thanks. Hear me?

MARINA: No thanks Mamma.

MARGUERITE: I don't understand –

MARINA: Lee – tell me what it is? I don't sit in it do I?

LEE: I want you to understand right here and now – to stop giving
me and Marina gifts – can you afford them? No Sir you can't.
I'll give her what is necessary, the best I can do.

MARGUERITE: I was trying Lee –

MARINA: Is it for the baby? I've never seen a thing like that –

LEE: Hear what she says – I'll translate – she don't even know
what it is for! Listen to me – because today or tomorrow you
take sick and you spend all your money on us – I will have to
take care of you. Now come on Mamma I ain't going to take
care of you when I've got thirty dollars a week am I? Fact is
too – I don't have thirty dollars a week right now –

MARGUERITE: We'll go out – right now – we'll find a job – you
and I – there's this woman at the Texas employment agency –
don't you recall how she was ever calling you on up – and say
I got this job and that job?

LEE: But Marina –

MARGUERITE: We won't be long. I'll help you find a job – right
now – right now you see –

LEE: Mamma I'll find a job – my way –

MARGUERITE: You'll find one – with me – and we'll buy cakes – but right now with me – in my car.

LEE: Why do I always go? I was stronger about you when I was a kid – I'd say go to hell Mamma – and don't come back any . . .

MARGUERITE: I'm waiting . . .

(*She taps her foot.* LEE *suddenly seems cowed. He doesn't want to go. But he does. He pulls a short jerkin from a chair. Slowly so slowly he puts it on.*)

LEE: Marina . . .

(*He kisses her briefly. She looks up at him.*)

We won't be gone long . . .

(*They both leave. A door slams shut somewhere.* MARINA *picks up a large rag doll and sits it in front of the highchair. She faces the highchair towards the television set. She switches the set on. The sound comes on. It is the Gregory Peck movie. June in the next room begins to cry. She cries some more.* MARINA *goes over to a table, pulls out a packet of cigarettes from under the table. They are glued under the table with chewing gum. She unsticks the gum, and takes out a cigarette. June cries louder.* MARINA *increases the sound from the movie. She sits back and watches the noisy television.*

Darkness again. Fade Out.

The stage is dark. MARINA *walks to the front of the stage. A spot picks up her face. The voice from the audience carries on as if there has been no interruption.*)

COMMISSION: When you moved to Dallas where did you live the first time?

MARINA: I did not move to Dallas together with Lee. Lee went to Dallas when he found the job, and I remained in Fort Worth and lived with Elena Hall.

COMMISSION: For how long a period did you live with Mrs Hall?

MARINA: I think that it was about a month and a half.

COMMISSION: During that month and a half what did your husband do?

MARINA: He had a job. He was working. He would call me up over the telephone but how he spent his time, I don't know.

COMMISSION: Do you know during that month and a half where he lived?

MARINA: At first I know that he rented a room in the YMCA but very shortly thereafter he rented an apartment. But where I don't know.

COMMISSION: During that month and a half did he come to see you and the baby?

MARINA: Yes two or three times he came to see us because he had no car. It was not very easy.

COMMISSION: After this month and a half did he find a place for you all to live together?

MARINA: Yes but it wasn't a problem there to find a place, no problem there to find a place.

COMMISSION: Did you then move to a home in Dallas?

MARINA: Yes, on Elsbeth Street in Dallas.

COMMISSION: Did you observe any guns in your things when you moved?

MARINA: No.

COMMISSION: Did you have a telephone there?

MARINA: No.

COMMISSION: What about his reading habits there – were they the same?

MARINA: Yes about the same.

COMMISSION: Can you tell us a little more fully about his reading? Did he spend several hours each evening in this reading?

MARINA: Yes.

COMMISSION: Do you recall any of the books that he read at Elsbeth Street?

MARINA: No. He had two books, two thick books on the history of the United States.

COMMISSION: Did you go out in the evenings?

MARINA: Yes.

COMMISSION: Where did you go?

MARINA: Sometimes we went shopping to stores, and movies, though Lee really went to the movies himself. He wanted to take me but I did not understand English. Then on weekends we would go to a lake not far away or to a park or to the cafe for some ice-cream.

COMMISSION: Were either you or your husband taking any schooling at that time?

MARINA: Lee took English courses or typing courses . . .

COMMISSION: About what time would he get home from work?

MARINA: About 5 to 5.30.

COMMISSION: Then would you eat your evening meal?

MARINA: Yes.

COMMISSION: How soon after that would he leave for the class?

MARINA: When Lee took his courses he generally did not come home for dinner, usually he didn't.

COMMISSION: Did he practise his typewriting at home at all?

MARINA: At home no. But he had a book, a textbook on typing which he would review when he was at home.

COMMISSION: How soon after the class was over did he come home ordinarily?

MARINA: Nine o'clock.

COMMISSION: Did he tell you anything about friends that he met at these classes?

MARINA: No.

COMMISSION: While you were at Elsbeth Street do you recall seeing any guns in your apartment?

MARINA: No.

COMMISSION: When did you move to Neely Street from the Elsbeth Street apartment?

MARINA: In January after the New Year. I don't remember exactly.

COMMISSION: Do you remember why you moved from Elsbeth Street to Neely Street?

MARINA: I liked it better on Neely Street. We had a porch there. And that was more convenient for the child.

COMMISSION: Did you have any differences with your husband while you were at Neely Street?

MARINA: No. Well there are always some reasons for some quarrel between a husband and wife, not everything is always smooth.

COMMISSION: I had in mind if there was any violence or any hitting of you. Did that occur at Neely Street?

MARINA: No. That was on Elsbeth Street.

COMMISSION: Do you recall what brought that about?

MARINA: Not quite. I am trying to remember. It seems to me that it was at that time that Lee began to talk about his wanting to return to Russia. I did not want that and that is why we had quarrels.

COMMISSION: Did you have discussions between you about this idea of returning to Russia?

MARINA: Yes. Lee wanted me to . . .

(*She steps back into the stage.*

The lights rise up. LEE *is in the room with her on Elsbeth Street. There is a cot near the wall, beside an open window. He is talking agitatedly.*)

LEE: . . . I've been considering – Marina – now I've been considering –

MARINA: You say that twice –

LEE: What I said before when I said –

MARINA: Only say I said –

LEE: My Russian isn't good!

MARINA: Shout!

LEE: I ain't – I'm breathing – don't you see – you needle me some.

MARINA: Do I? What about Lee – dear Lee –

LEE: Oh come on! You know I hate that sort of stuff –

MARINA: Then – I was only joking. I wasn't making a pass at you –

LEE: That's what I mean Marina.

MARINA: It's very difficult to know what you ever mean –

LEE: I mean if you're loving sometimes it was a joke and if you are not loving it still is – and I don't know you. I don't. We're not here – you talk in Russian with me Marina like this and all – isn't it a game? A sort of way of living? Not – living.

MARINA: I don't understand you Lee.

LEE: As I was saying before I got interrupted – I was saying what I mean – I was saying.

MARINA: You said –

LEE: Will you listen! Once in my life – will you let me – I'll tell it and well Marina I'll say it all well in good Russian if you'll stop – there now.

(*They stare at each other. He finds it difficult to say what comes into his mind.*)

You stop? For Lee?

MARINA: I stop you stop he stop –

LEE: I want you to go on back . . . it all can't be the same as it was . . . I remember snow and the cold, things like lines for potatoes because the crop stay down in the earth and no one no matter how he try get it up out of the grass . . . that was Minsk Marina.

MARINA: I forget it –

LEE: Sure you do. But that's as how it was. This is no place here now what is all this if it ain't another kind of poverty – it's warm, fruit is cheap –

MARINA: Then you like it.

LEE: It's a desert. Nothing nurtures. There is no reality you don't feel the rest of the world and all its problems come crowding in on this room here –

MARINA: Do I have to Lee?

LEE: Texas thinks only about Texas. Ask a Texan where all those Russkies come from he don't know – he'll tell you they come from off of the moon or something like and they going hit us with red flying saucers from up there – hey!

MARINA: Yes Lee.

LEE: No Lee! . . . Marina, you go back . . .

MARINA: And line for potatoes – are you mad – I sometime wonder if I am not understanding the language – but you are!

LEE: It would be better –

MARINA: Make sense Lee! If you send me away you don't love me.

LEE: I do of course but –

MARINA: You lie.

LEE: No Marina.

MARINA: And I not come back? Have I a chance to ever come back again?

LEE: I'll join you – but later – I must have time –

MARINA: How do I know that?

LEE: You don't. Trust.

MARINA: After we have come ten thousand miles – how can I possibly ever go back? If you want me to go – you never loved right from the start. I did.

LEE: Perhaps we have both forgot the loving – if it was there anyway. But you're going back to Russia. I say you are.

MARINA: Give me one good reason?

LEE: It just would be better that way.

MARINA: What would – what in the name of God would!

LEE: We mustn't shout – the baby.

MARINA: I'll shout.

(LEE *hits her in the mouth with a half-closed fist.* MARINA *grabs his arm and tries to kick back at him.*)

LEE: No.

MARINA: And I'm a woman too!

LEE: I want you to go on home –

MARINA: I won't – you see I defeat you – I stay silent I say nothing. I won't talk about it. It is forgotten – wiped off. I say nothing. You hit me you see – I say nothing.

(LEE *hits her again in the chest.* MARINA *grips her breast. She is hurt. She won't shout.*)

LEE: Nothing works Marina – not ever – now you'll go – won't you?

(*He hits her. She falls back on the bed. She refuses to speak.*)

You'll say you will – or I'll do it again –

(*She shakes her head furiously.*)

You'll say it and you'll say it – and you'll go back home!

(*He hits her on her face, on her neck, on her shoulders. She holds her hand to her mouth to stop herself screaming.*)

Let the child wake up – you both go –

(MARINA *stuffs a piece of the cotton bedspread into her mouth so that she cannot scream.*

LEE *stops hitting her. She shakes a little. She lies where she falls on the bed.* LEE *sits crosslegged in a corner. He stares at her.*)

. . . you know Marina . . . I don't think you ever loved me at all . . . I didn't believe you when you said it in Minsk – I mean I was already in love with somebody else Marina – you came along – but isn't it just possible between you and me neither of us had much love – you call it love, Mamma calls it love – but it's a way of jealousy and possession and I can't abide none of that now . . . If you only did what I said once – were not so lazy – if you once played ball – I'd come back to you – wherever you are. In New York when I was at junior high they began to call me Ossie Rabbit – now they said Ossie was for Oswald, and I kept popping up in strange places so that when they saw me peep over a wall to see the gang there – they'd say there goes Ossie Rabbit. I remember . . . Marina you're not listening any . . . Marina . . . now Marina what if that baby ups and starts . . .

(*We dim the stage again. His voice fades. It is black once more. From the gloom* MARGUERITE *steps forward. It is obvious she has been talking for some time. She appears to be in mid paragraph.*)

MARGUERITE: . . . . It has been stated in the paper that my son was giving Marina black eyes and possibly had beat her. And this is by the Russian people. Now living in this home in Fort Worth, I had gone by several times I had a day off, and Marina was not at home. I said to her Marina, Mamma come to see you yesterday. You no home. She didn't answer. I said Marina Mamma come see you. You no home. Marina. No. I go to lady's house to take English lessons.

COMMISSION: Do you know who she was speaking of?

MARGUERITE: I do not know for a fact. But my son Robert will know. And that is why it is important to call him. That is what I am trying to say Chief Justice Warren. These others will know this part of my story, give you the facts. I am assuming it is Mr Peter Gregory's wife that started these lessons. But Marina was taking English lessons. Now, they lived at a corner house, and there is Carol Street, and opposite Carol Street is a parking lot for Montgomery Ward. They live approximately two blocks from Montgomery Ward. So I had gone by, as I am stating, several times. You have to understand – this is just six or seven weeks that they are in this home.

COMMISSION: You say 'they'. I am sorry to interrupt.

MARGUERITE: Marina and Lee in this home . . . Then Marina was not home. I could not understand where so fast that they could have so many friends, that this Russian girl didn't speak English and know her way about, could be gone all day long. That worried me. So I sat in the car on Montgomery Ward's parking lot, where I could see the house, because I wanted to see who Marina was going to come home with. The door was open. I went in the house and no one was there. But this time, I was wondering how she could be gone all the time, being a stranger in town. I sat in the car all day long. She didn't show up. Finally I went home, had my supper, left my apartment, and on the way going back to the house Lee was leaving Montgomery Ward. He got in the car with me and we had about a block to go. I entered the home with Lee, and I said – Lee, where is Marina? Of course, I knew that she wasn't home, because I had stayed in the car all day. He said – oh I guess she is out with some friends. Would you like me to fix your supper? No. She will probably be home in time to fix my supper. And I left. I'm not going to interfere in their married life. But I did offer to fix him supper. And I went back to make sure Marina still wasn't home. I walked in the home with my son. So approximately two days later – not approximately, but two days later, I went to the home and my son was reading, he read continuously – in the living-room, and Marina was in the bedroom. I could not see Marina. And I said to Lee –

(*The lights come up again.* LEE *sits front stage.* MARINA *her back turned away is on a bed back stage. There is a strained silence.* MARGUERITE *stares at* LEE *uncertainly.*)

MARGUERITE: Lee then?

LEE: Yes Mamma?

MARGUERITE: You could smile some –

LEE: Say what you want Mamma.

MARGUERITE: You don't want to talk?

LEE: Been talking – just right now.

MARGUERITE: What kind of?

LEE: Just talk.

MARGUERITE: Politics?

LEE: No sir.

MARGUERITE: Philosophics?

LEE: Now no.

MARGUERITE: There's only one thing you two ever can sit down and talk about.

LEE: We are not quarrelling Mamma.

MARGUERITE: It's very silent – like an icebox.

LEE: Iceboxes'll hum Mamma – you know like – bbbrrrrrhhh.

MARGUERITE: Because I'm only ever thinking of helping –

LEE: Yes.

MARGUERITE: It seems strange when I sees people not talking when God gives tongues –

LEE: No reason to talk any more Mamma when you come in – you talk enough for three –

MARGUERITE: That I do when my mind's made up –

LEE: But the baby must have quiet see.

MARGUERITE: Is that a historical philosophic book you are reading?

LEE: Biography of George Washington.

MARGUERITE: Tell Marina I am here.

(LEE *ignores her and reads his book.* MARINA *sits like a piece of George Segal in white plaster. Turned away just that little bit.*)
Lee?

(LEE *reads. He shrinks lower in his chair.*)
Marina? (*She crosses the stage. To* MARINA) . . . Marina baby – it's Mamma.

(MARINA *turns around. She is nursing young June. June is a white swathe of cloth. She has a markedly clear black eye. She has bruises on her face.*

MARGUERITE *tries to touch* MARINA. MARINA *stands away. She genuflects back from* MARGUERITE.)

MARGUERITE: Baby – who did that?

(MARINA *doesn't understand.* MARGUERITE *points out the mark on* MARINA's *face.*)

MARINA: Mamma – Lee.

MARGUERITE: When honey?

MARINA: Mamma – Lee.

(*Something doll-like and pathetic about* MARINA *this time. She is utterly bewildered, she doesn't know her surroundings or her friends.* MARGUERITE *walks back up front.*)

MARGUERITE: Lee – what do you mean?

LEE: Come again?

MARGUERITE: Striking Marina?

LEE: Oh that . . .

MARGUERITE: Tell me.

LEE: Mother – that is our affair.

MARGUERITE: But I think you are a louse for it. I may know what goes on but there is no need to hit the girl.

(LEE *ignores* MARGUERITE. *He is talking to* MARINA *in Russian.* MARGUERITE *doesn't understand them.*)

LEE: Mamma says she been watching you – Marina? What do you say?

MARGUERITE: Lee – I was addressing you in English I was –

LEE: What do you say Marina?

MARINA: Mamma would.

LEE: Yearh she would – I can just see – and all – following you on down the street and saying now just why does she stay inside that house all the day?

MARINA: I told you Lee.

LEE: Sure. Mamma knows. You go see Paul Gregory for those English lessons – and it all makes sense.

MARINA: Russian lessons! He said he wanted to learn Russian –

LEE: And he's a nice good-looking all American – and he wants to further his mind – what about that? (*He turns savagely on* MARGUERITE) . . . And when I want to broaden my mind Mamma – what do they say – he's a nut! Give him ten dollars a day, and a few straight words from the John Birch Society and he's all fixed up ready to die – what is it Mamma that makes me not want to be this year's automobile? The model, which, when you buy it, you can't even afford to sell it secondhand because the price don't cover the credit tag! What is it about America when you can't afford to live in it, and I hear – now, cost of dying is so high the Lord's fixing on his own insurance scheme! (*He turns back to* MARINA. *He is speaking in Russian*) And who's a clean-cut all American boy! What is it I ought to give you because now you've a nice young foreign friend? An English lesson! You want an English education – that kind of education is the same language in the same bed all over the world!

MARINA: You're shouting Lee.

LEE: No I'm not. I'm just holding my mouth a little more open.

MARGUERITE: Lee – I have already spoken to Marina –

LEE: So have I –

MARGUERITE: You have hit her not –

LEE: I always thought – Marina – you came to me – like I was always here – and I thought I'd teach Marina English and Marina would show me Russian – and it would always be a fair mutual honest exchange –

MARGUERITE: Lee you're not listening to me none – now what I came to see and I wouldn't have said it unless my conscience pricked me – seeing you two fighting –

LEE: Somehow – dead or alive Mamma – the last word is always yours.

MARGUERITE: I was saying! Dammit! How is it Marina says she goes for English lessons to the young man – when his family says it is Russian lessons Marina give him – and all the day long I stand there and see too well – Marina don't come home! Explain me that?

LEE: Because Mamma – it must be, my English ain't that good enough.

MARGUERITE: For her?

(*The stage blackens. There is a pause in time.*
The darkness is relieved by a spot which picks up the shape of MARINA. *She comes forward to the audience. She seems composed.*
She waits until the COMMISSIONER *puts his questions. But she has been answering his questions all day.*)

COMMISSION: Did you observe some time when you thought he changed?

MARINA: I would say that immediately after coming to the United States Lee changed. I did not know him as such a man in Russia.

COMMISSION: Will you describe how you observed these changes and what they were as you saw them?

MARINA: He helped me as before but he became a little more of a recluse. He did not like my Russian friends and he tried to forbid me to have anything to do with them. He was very irritable, sometimes for a trifle, for a trifling reason.

COMMISSION: Did he tell you why he did not like your Russian friends?

MARINA: I don't know why he didn't like them. I didn't understand. At least that which he said was completely unfounded. He simply said some stupid or foolish things.

COMMISSION: Will you tell us the stupid things that he said?

MARINA: Well, he thought that they were fools for having left Russia; they were all traitors. I would tell him he was in the same position being an American in America but there were really no reasons just irritation. He said that they all only like money, and everything is measured by money. It seems to me that perhaps he was envious of them in the sense they were more prosperous than he was. When I told him, when I would say that to him he did not like to hear that. Perhaps I shouldn't say these foolish things and I feel kind of uncomfortable to talk about the foolish things that happened or what he said foolish things. This is one of the reasons why I don't really know the reasons for these quarrels because sometimes these quarrels were just trifles. It is just that Lee was very unrestrained and very explosive at that time.

COMMISSION: Mrs Oswald, we will ask you to be very frank with us. It isn't for the purpose of embarrassing you or your husband that we ask you these things but it might help us to understand and even if you will tell us the foolish and stupid things it may shed some light on the problem. You understand that?

MARINA: I understand that you are not asking these questions out of curiosity but for a reason.

COMMISSION: Did your husband indicate any particular Russian friends that he disliked more than others?

MARINA: He liked de Mohrenschildt but he – because he was a strong person, but only de Mohrenschildt. He did not like Bouhe or Anna Meller.

COMMISSION: Did you ever tell him you liked these people?

MARINA: Yes. I told him all the time that I liked these people and that is why he was angry at me and would tell me that I was just like they were. At one time I left him and went to my friends because he put me into – put me on the spot by saying – well if you like your friends so much then go ahead and live with them. And he left me no choice.

COMMISSION: When was this Mrs Oswald?

MARINA: On Elsbeth Street.

COMMISSION: How long were you gone from him then?

MARINA: One week.

COMMISSION: Did he ask you to return?

MARINA: Yes. I took June and I went to Anna Meller, took a cab and went there. I spent several days with her. Lee didn't know where I was but he called up and about two or three days after I came to and we met at de Mohrenschildt's house and he asked me to return home. I, of course, did not want a divorce but I told him it would be better to get a divorce rather than to continue living and quarrelling this way. After all this is only a burden on a man if two people live together and fight. I simply wanted to show him too, that I am not a toy. That a woman is a little more complicated. That you cannot trifle with her.

COMMISSION: Did you say anything at that time about how he should treat you if you returned?

MARINA: Yes. I told him if he did not change his character, then it would become impossible to continue living with him. Because if there should be such quarrels continuously that would be crippling for the children.

COMMISSION: What did he say to that?

MARINA: Then he said that it would be – it was very hard for him. That he could not change. That I must accept him, such as he was. And he asked me to come back home with him right on that day but he left feeling bad because I did not go and remained with my friend.

COMMISSION: Then did he get in touch with you again?

MARINA: At that time there was very little room at Anna Meller's and it was very uncomfortable and I left and went to Katya Ford whose husband at that time happened to be out of town on business. I spent several days with Katya Ford but then when her husband returned I did not want to remain with her. And it was on a Sunday morning then when I moved over to Anna Ray. Lee called me and said he wanted to see me and he came that evening . . .

(*The lights come up.* MARINA *walks back into the stage.* LEE *is looking curiously around. They talk in Russian.* MARINA *is artificially calm.* LEE *is troubled but sort of witty about things.*)

LEE: Which hotel is this?

MARINA: She is a kind of friend of mine she let me stay –

LEE: So was Katya.

MARINA: Yes.

LEE: So was Anna Meller.

MARINA: But I chose to come here.

LEE: Throw you out did they?

MARINA: I chose to.

LEE: Run out of friends soon Marina.

MARINA: You already have. Who do I have to turn to – I must make my own.

LEE: Funny how they're not mine – not a dickhead there is a friend of mine –

MARINA: They are married women – who have families – they also have . . .

(*She won't say. She cuts her tongue off.*)

LEE: Have what?

MARINA: I was going to say – husbands.

LEE: You mean like a lover not a husband –

MARINA: He should be both!

LEE: This one ain't.

MARINA: There was a time –

LEE: Now why do women always go back – into the past – there was there was – but I'm here now honey.

MARINA: I'm not hungry. You can have what's on my plate –

LEE: Like it's a dog what crawls in – and you feed it?

MARINA: Just sit down – be calm – if you don't want it –

LEE: I do. (*He sits at the table.* MARINA *fetches him some bread*) . . . Nice place. Does she pay the rent and all? Or –

MARINA: She's a nice woman –

LEE: Yearh? Where do you sleep?

MARINA: That's a funny question.

LEE: I don't ever ask you where you sleep do I?

MARINA: No.

LEE: As if I don't really want to know?

MARINA: Yes.

LEE: I do. I really do. It's interesting. It's always fine and satisfactory to know just where your wife is sleeping case comes a bad night and you ain't got no bunk yourself – says I.

(MARINA *stands smiling at him. He eats only a little.*)

I'd like to see sleeping – that's a waste of time – and eating – do you realize three meals a day, half an hour at breakfast, an hour and a half at luncheon and two hours in the evening time – what is that?

MARINA: I can't count that far.

LEE: I can – you rely on Decimals Lee you're one straight goodies man – that is – eh, four hours daily and it's got to go – now in four hours you could have written a sonnet, launched an ICBM or –

MARINA: Become a better man?

(LEE *sits and stares and thinks. It takes time. He decides he doesn't like it any. It's a crack.*)

LEE: Cut that out. Who's been talking at you?

MARINA: Nobody, Lee.

LEE: All that you can cut out –

MARINA: I'm sorry –

LEE: There's no butter!

MARINA: I'll get some –

LEE: That's not the point – what for do you bring bread and then there is no butter to go on the bread. This ain't no Minsk is it now!

MARINA: Lee I forgot –

LEE: It's that it's only Lee – that half shot-off husband come to bore all you all to all hell death – give Ossie Rabbit the bones!

MARINA: You're being impossible –

LEE: I'm saying it's symbolic. Where's the butter Marina – where's the cream on the top of the milk that old great society milk fed – what do you want a new car?

MARINA: I don't want anything that I have to ask for.

LEE: Oldsmobile?

MARINA: The joke is over –

LEE: Not a Ford – not a showy Caddie – you want a Stingray – you want a Corvette –

(MARINA *goes into the kitchen. She comes back with a plate of butter.* LEE *is still provoking. She places it on the table in front of him.*)

Then in great American hardware stores – you find a plastic foodmix, or a chromium icebox or a record-player or even buy a long-playing record of music 'for people who don't want to waste their time listening to music anyway'! How about that –

(*He sees the butter. He throws it across the floor.*)

MARINA: I just brought you it Lee!

LEE: Lee's changed his mind.

MARINA: Lee – you're insane!

LEE: Don't ever say that – I see clear as sunlight I see I do!

MARINA: You asked for butter –

LEE: Now I don't want it!

MARINA: . . . what is it? What can I do? I have never known by night or day – what it is you want? . . .

(LEE *is stopped at that sad sound in her voice.*)

LEE: A way.

MARINA: Where?

LEE: To understand.

MARINA: Understand what?

LEE: A way to understand . . . that's all.

(MARINA *scoops up the butter carefully. He is on his knees helping her.*)

MARINA: You're not helping me Lee – you keep putting your knees in the butter while I –

LEE: I want you back home –

MARINA: No.

LEE: Yes. It's gonna be. It doesn't work any other way –

MARINA: Not for all the shouting –

LEE: I'm like that. Aren't I? I don't breathe right when you're gone –

MARINA: You have no one to shout at?

LEE: I can't – I won't want to live any more than now – if you don't. I don't have anything else. Sure I loathe it. I haven't the collateral the way to live with money – I don't even know where money is – what it looks like – I boasted about America in Minsk – now I'm ashamed I don't give you

America – America is two rooms and a cold-water place and I'm sorry – if it were different you'd be happier oh I know . . .

MARINA: You really want me to go back –

LEE: Home.

MARINA: No. You really mean I go back to Russia –

LEE: I mean to Neely Street with me –

MARINA: No. Say what you first said. I must go home. What you said remember – Marina go back to Russia I'll feel better you can get work there and I'll join you –

LEE: I don't mean that –

MARINA: You only say what you partially mean you only do what you need to do Lee – say it all do it all in one.

LEE: Marina I have nothing I am nothing – I am awfully alone. I won't talk about Russia – just accept I am as you see me. Will you come on home? And bring June?

MARINA: Not for a while . . .

LEE: I won't shout none . . .

MARINA: But if I want to see my friends –

LEE: I'll say nothing. I'm begging you now – don't make me beg.

MARINA: And I'll smoke when I want.

LEE: If you must.

MARINA: You won't call me lazy or – what is the word – slut?

LEE: You'll come back?

MARINA: . . . yes Lee.

> (*The stage darkens again. Their voices and their movements are swallowed up in the slow dark night.*
>
> *A spot fixes on* MARGUERITE. *She is a little more estranged from us. She is still talking and defending her son. She sees him as no other person close can see him. Yet the picture of him is so diffuse. She walks forward on the stage.*)

COMMISSION: . . . Did he ever talk about re-enlisting into the Marines after he returned?

MARGUERITE: Well, when Lee returned he was with me three days, and then of course, he went over to visit Robert's house. So actually we didn't talk.

COMMISSION: He said nothing about re-enlisting in the Marines?

MARGUERITE: No. The three days he was home. That was the

conversation – about him going on a ship. I saw his passport. And his passport was stamped 'import and export' on his passport.

COMMISSION: Did you know that he spoke Russian at that time, when he had the passport?

MARGUERITE: No sir I did not know . . . Now one thing I have forgotten. While at the State Department, the State Department told me that Lee had gone to Finland before Russia. And I did not know that. Now, Lee had applied at a college in Finland, evidently, because on the application it states such a fact. I did not know – because the paper just said he arrived in Russia – (*She waves a large white sheet of paper at the audience*) . . . This is Lee's original application, that you cannot possibly have had. This is the only application there is. So this is something new for you gentlemen. I am not going to go through it all, because you have a copy. But I am going to show you the thinking of this young man. Special interests: religious, vocational, literary, sports and hobbies. Philosophy, psychology, ideology, football, baseball, tennis, stamp collecting. Lee had a stamp collecting book. Nature of private reading: Jack London, Darwin, Norman Vincent Peale, scientific books, philosophy and so on.

(*On the other side of the stage a spot picks up* MARINA's *face. She is further away from the front than her mother-in-law. She repeats a phrase she has already said.*)

MARINA: . . . It seemed peculiar to me and didn't want to believe it but he did not love his mother, she was not quite a normal woman. Now, I know this for sure.

(*The spot fades.* MARGUERITE *is still talking. The light is still on her.*)

COMMISSION: You think that he decided to defect after this application?

MARGUERITE: I do not know sir because I have not had this from the boy. I am speculating. But I have a lot of documents to sustain my speculation.

COMMISSION: Now, this, you cannot tell one way or another about whether he is an agent by this?

MARGUERITE: I cannot tell by anything he is an agent, if you want proof. I am becoming a little discouraged about this, because I keep telling you – I did not have proof, sir. But I am giving you documents leading to it.

COMMISSION: All that I am trying to find out is what you have. You are giving us that. I am also trying to find out whatever proof you have about these various things that we can rely on.

MARGUERITE: Well I am going to state once and for all, because it upsets me very much emotionally. And I have stated before, I do not have proof, sir. I do not have proof of an agent. I do not have proof my son is innocent. I do not have proof.

COMMISSION: You don't have any proof of a conspiracy?

MARGUERITE: Of anything. It is just as I feel, like the Dallas Police do not have proof my son shot President Kennedy. If they have anything, it is circumstantial evidence. I have as much circumstantial evidence here that Lee was an agent as the Dallas police have that he shot President Kennedy.

ACT TWO

The stage is dark once more. Out of the black stillness on the stage
MARINA *steps forward as the voice begins the questions again.*

    The spot picks up her young rather pretty but certainly very American-
ized features. She is very well dressed. In a sense one feels she is be-
having too well. Her poise and compliance don't add up to her whole
being.

COMMISSION: Could you tell us those things that you observed
    that caused you to think he had something in mind at that
    time, and I will ask you later, after you tell us, those that you
    discovered since or that you have obtained more light on
    since.

MARINA: At that time I did not think anything about it. I had no
    reasons to think that he had something in mind. I did not
    understand him at that time.

COMMISSION: Do you recall the first time that you observed the
    rifle?

MARINA: That was on Neely Street. I think that was in February
    1963.

COMMISSION: How did you learn about it? Did you see it some
    place in the apartment?

MARINA: Yes, Lee had a small room where he spent a great deal of
    time, where he read – where he kept his things, and that is
    where the rifle was.

COMMISSION: Was it out in the room at that time, as dis-
    tinguished from in a closet in the room?

MARINA: Yes it was open, out in the open. At first I think – I saw
    some package up on the top shelf, and I think that that
    was the rifle. But I didn't know. And apparently later he

assembled it and had it in the room.

COMMISSION: When you saw the rifle assembled in the room, did it have the scope on it?

MARINA: No it did not have a scope on it.

COMMISSION: Did you have any discussion with your husband about the rifle when you first saw it?

MARINA: Of course I asked him . . .

(*The lights come up.* LEE *is on the floor on his knees. He has gun grease and polish and a barrel plunger before him. The gun is in pieces.*

LEE *is in a small room. A door is near to his arm.* MARINA *stands in the doorway looking down on him. He doesn't seem surprised. Then after she talks to him he becomes surprised and truculent. They talk in Russian.*)

MARINA: . . . Haven't I seen that before?

LEE: Depends . . . if you've been in and around here in my room – then you been smelling some haven't you? I mean by that – you been looking – and – Marina – in my room.

MARINA: I saw a parcel – last week –

LEE: But you looked inside my room. You only saw a parcel because you only could have seen a parcel if you had opened that door and peered in.

MARINA: So?

LEE: So . . . eh – you been peering in on my private life – my room that is.

MARINA: I'm sorry –

LEE: Too late.

MARINA: Lock it if you don't want me to see –

LEE: I don't.

MARINA: Buy a lock.

LEE: Can't afford it any.

MARINA: How much did that thing cost Lee?

LEE: If you had seen fit to understand how a man is – you'd know you don't just bust in on his private room – my room – and you'd know it is loyalty that keeps it that way. Like I say. It's trust Marina . . .

MARINA: How much Lee?

LEE: If you had trust Marina –

(MARINA *pulls his hair. She is very serious.*)

MARINA: What did I ask you?

LEE: And that's no good – didn't I say my hair was falling out – and you come and pull it! Now what quicker way to have a man's hair all fall out than pull it Marina – !
(MARINA *stands and waits and watches on him.*)
. . . It cost twenty-one dollars.

MARINA: Why?

LEE: Why? Because 'why' the rifle costs money? You know it costs money!

MARINA: Why buy it? We're poor. I'd like – that money, thank you. June would. Wouldn't she like shoes? And you buy that!

LEE: I had one before –

MARINA: Russia's different –

LEE: There's hunting – handy for some hunting out of town –

MARINA: That's not the point! You tell me Lee how much things cost! A refrigerator costs that rifle, does it?

LEE: If you like – a very old one that is –

MARINA: A suit for me and shoes and stockings – how much?

LEE: I can't talk to you.

MARINA: And you buy this thing – and you polish it!

LEE: I said not to interfere in my private things – there's squirrel and ducktail out there – that's all.

MARINA: Then I won't ask you any more.

LEE: Fine – well then you'll excuse me some.

MARINA: Is the rifle more interesting . . . ?

LEE: I thought I told you never to pull at my hair – that's what made me mad – now you're sore –

MARINA: No –

LEE: Putting it on me that you are –

MARINA: I – I can't understand you Lee – I try –

LEE: All I want is to be left see.

MARINA: And you don't love June and I –

LEE: I do. I told you I do.

MARINA: I'm trying to say – you are so different now.

LEE: Of course I am. When you do something that throws me yes I am. First it was my room – then it was pulling on my hair – and then, now, I mean – I remember other things which

187

make life more difficult for me –

MARINA: Remember what?

LEE: Didn't I get out – by telling you you pulled at my hair – I recall when I bought that bottle of restorer –

MARINA: I don't understand you I don't understand you!

LEE: For my hair! Because – because it was falling out – I put it on the side table – and you fed June – and I was coming in and I saw you clear as day – try put that hair grease from that bottle – my restorer bottle – on June's rusk and you say what is it that has changed!

MARINA: But I didn't put that restorer on June's –

LEE: But I'm saying I thought you were then going on and about to put it!

(MARINA *is suddenly exhausted.*)

MARINA: Yes Lee.

LEE: And I'm saying I wouldn't have recalled the bad things if you hadn't have brought them up by saying you been spying on me some.

MARINA: I'm tired now . . . too much shouting . . .

LEE: She is lazy and slow and she won't cook but she wants refrigerators and now she's tired and all!

MARINA: Can I . . . do something for you. Can I do anything. I will. I apologize. I forget all about what I'm supposed to have done . . . Can I? Anything now I'll do – ?

LEE: Now you're being cowardly.

MARINA: Name something –

LEE: All right. But no more games.

MARINA: No.

LEE: Ask me nothing . . . I must breathe I must have a corner . . . here is another thing . . . (*He goes to a drawer. He pulls out an Imperial reflex camera. He hands it to her*) Now I been putting all this together – like it is now – now you come out here – and I'll pose you. I'll pose for you and you take a picture – because I have another thing you must see – (*He opens another drawer. He pulls out a gun and a holster*) . . . I bought this too. Now this is a much better gun. The rifle is here – and it's ready and everything – and I put the gun on – and you come over here – (*He pulls her out to the front of the stage. He strikes a pose just like the Commission picture shows. And* MARINA *gingerly holds up the camera*) Yes you are. It's loaded. Now come on. Wind it up to a new number – have you? Now – where's the sun Marina?

MARINA: Behind me.

LEE: That's the first right thing you haven't done wrong all day –!
(MARINA *takes two pictures. Click. Then rewind. Click.*)
I was thinking – you know what it was? There was June – eating that hair restorer – as if you'd given it to her – and I had a dream about it – I had a dream – she ate it I always remember these things in retrospection – that's a long word – I hope it's right – I ain't never had it right in English – and I dreamt all her teeth – that is June's – came out all growing sprouting out with hairs and she looked like a walrus and she said –
(MARINA *begins to laugh.*)
What is funny Marina?

MARINA: I'm laughing that's all –
(*She laughs out loud as if from great relief. As if some way of looking at* LEE *came clear to her.*)

LEE: I don't see why you should laugh – I have a serious psychological thing about hair and teeth – and hair and teeth are symbols of psychological importance –
(MARINA *is still laughing.*)

MARINA: Lee . . . I can't hold the camera.

LEE: And I know I'm worried . . . about decay and growth – and the fall of civilizations and . . .
(*He just stares at her laughing.*)

MARINA: I can't help it . . . it's so impossible to understand you – oh . . . I'm really crying. Laughing and crying you see . . .
(LEE *still adopts his silly militaristic pose. He looks very wary and uncertain and slightly silly. As indeed* MARINA *sees him. She laughs and wipes her eyes.*)

LEE: If you would kindly tell me what's funny Marina – I'd laugh too maybe.

MARINA: You couldn't . . . oh you couldn't. That's what's so funny!
(*The stage falls away into blackness. No figures are distinguishable. Her laughter and* LEE'S *strained surprise filter away. After a*

moment MARINA *comes back up front. Her face is made clear by the spotlight. The voice asks her questions.*)

COMMISSION: Did you have anything to do with the prints of the photograph after the prints were made? That is, did you put them in a photograph album yourself?

MARINA: Lee gave me one photograph and asked me to keep it for June somewhere. Of course June doesn't need photographs like that.

COMMISSION: Do you recall how long after that the Walker matter occurred?

MARINA: Two perhaps three weeks later. I don't know. You know better when this happened.

COMMISSION: How did you first learn that your husband had shot at General Walker?

MARINA: That evening he went out, I thought that he had gone to his classes or perhaps that he just walked out or went out on his own business. It got to be about ten or ten thirty he wasn't home yet, and I began to be worried. Perhaps even later. Then I went into his room. Somehow – I was drawn to it – you know – I was pacing around. Then I saw a note there.

COMMISSION: Did you look for the gun at that time?

MARINA: No. I didn't understand anything. On the note it said – 'If I am arrested' and there are certain other questions such as for example, the key to the mailbox in such and such a place, and that he left me some money to last me for some time, and I couldn't understand at all what can he be arrested for. When he came back I asked him what had happened. He was very pale. I don't remember the exact time, but it was very late. And he told me not to ask him any questions. He only told me that he had shot at General Walker. Of course I didn't sleep all night. I thought that at any minute now the police will come. Of course I wanted to ask him a great deal. But in his state I decided I had best leave him alone – it would be purposeless to question him.

COMMISSION: Did he say any more than that about the shooting?

MARINA: Of course in the morning I told him that I was worried and that we can have a lot of trouble, and I asked him . . .

(*The lights come up again.* LEE *is in bed. He appears asleep.*

MARINA *walks across to the bed. She shakes the slumped shape of* LEE. *He stirs.*)

MARINA: . . . Lee?

LEE: . . . I'm asleep now.

MARINA: No . . . Lee!

LEE: You won't find out Marina – because you wouldn't understand any – so don't ask me . . .

MARINA: Where is the rifle?

LEE: You been snooping again –

MARINA: I looked in your room – and I looked under the bed –

LEE: Snooping some . . .

(MARINA *turns him out of bed. She rolls him and his blankets like a white cotton sausage across the floor.*)

MARINA: We'll all be killed we'll be thrown out – and we won't ever come back! Now speak to me!

(LEE *slowly disentangles himself from the sheets.*)

LEE: I hid it . . .

MARINA: Where?

LEE: Buried it . . .

MARINA: Did you kill the man?

LEE: You didn't – wait! – there, Marina, you didn't ask me where I buried the rifle.

MARINA: Oh – well?

LEE: I put it under trees and earth in the highway – in a back lot – where no dogs would smell it. Dogs can find an object anywhere – but earth – just damp natural and ordinary earth beats the smell.

MARINA: Kill kill!

LEE: No – I don't know – I guess I did – I don't know.

MARINA: And that's all?

LEE: You wouldn't understand any if I was to sit down and explain it – so I'm not going to waste my time Marina.

MARINA: You had no right –

LEE: No – but I did it.

MARINA: Why?

LEE: I tell you – like this – do you hear of the American Fact Finding Committee?

MARINA: No.

LEE: Hear of Mr Stevenson coming to Dallas?

MARINA: No.

LEE: Hear of people not wanting him to come?

MARINA: No.

LEE: Hear of fascists and fascism?

MARINA: Yes – they're bad people –

LEE: One mark! Out of a hundred! Hear of anti-semites? And of anti-communists?

MARINA: Yes and – no.

LEE: Then I can't tell you why.

MARINA: Why what?

LEE: I've just told you that's why – why what! – told you that's why what and you won't understand any because you just told me just now didn't you – you say no and no.

MARINA: You can't kill a man – because he thinks differently to you.

LEE: Did I kill him?

MARINA: I don't know.

LEE: But you just said –
(*He pulls pants over his pajama pants. Dresses hurriedly.*)

MARINA: I'm asking you Lee.

LEE: That's the point – I better go get a paper – did you hear the news on the radio?

MARINA: I'm too scared.

LEE: I'm going on out – get the papers. I'll be back.

MARINA: But Lee . . .
(LEE *stubs his feet into his shoes and leaves.*)

LEE: But Lee!

MARINA: Suppose he's dead!

LEE: Hell – I can't be that good a shot.
(*He runs out. The darkness descends on the stage.* MARINA *picks up a piece of white bed linen. She just stands holding it staring at it. After some moments,* MARINA *comes back up front. She is still answering questions. The single spotlight picks her up. It is obviously hard work and she is beginning to tire of questions and answer.*)

COMMISSION: After he shot at Walker, did you notice his taking the rifle out any more to practise?

MARINA: No.

COMMISSION: Do you recall when he went to New Orleans?

MARINA: I think it was in May. Lee went there himself, by himself. At that time, I became acquainted with Mrs Paine, and I stayed with her while he was looking for work. In about one week Lee telephoned me that he had found a job and that I should come down.

COMMISSION: Did you then leave at once for New Orleans?

MARINA: Yes.

COMMISSION: At New Orleans, who did your husband work for?

MARINA: He worked for the Louisiana Coffee Company. But I don't know in what capacity. I don't think that this was very good job, or perhaps more correctly, he did not – I know that he didn't like this job.

COMMISSION: How long did he work for this coffee company?

MARINA: I think it was from May until August, to the end of August.

COMMISSION: And then he was unemployed for a time?

MARINA: Yes.

(*The stage lightens.* LEE *is sitting very stiffly on a porch verandah in their flat. He holds his rifle between his knees. He just sits like a stone.* MARINA *is walking around, doing small things. She suddenly notices him there. She stands and stares strangely. He doesn't look at her. He doesn't move.*)

MARINA: Lee?

(*It is an early warm evening. The window to the porch is open. Warm summer sounds come in.*)

Lee – is that meant to be some kind of a joke?

LEE: No.

MARINA: Well why don't you come in?

LEE: I'm thinking.

MARINA: Oh.

LEE: You know – think like thought.

MARINA: I know Lee. Perhaps you'd tell me some of them?

LEE: I – no.

MARINA: Please Lee.

LEE: I was thinking about my books. But you never read them.

MARINA: I don't think that I was ever allowed to.

LEE: My books are about Washington, and Disraeli, and Kerensky – and then there's de Gaulle and Truman – now you don't read those books.

MARINA: What do they say Lee?

LEE: They show how a guy can become President – can show his country the way –

MARINA: Oh yes.

LEE: I'm going to find a way. I could become – it all takes time – but there is no reason why I shouldn't be President of the United States in twenty years.

MARINA: How?

LEE: I'm saying there ain't no reason – none at all –

MARINA: I don't understand –

LEE: There is no reason why I shouldn't –

MARINA: What reason Lee?

LEE: I'm saying there's no reason at all – that's all.

MARINA: But you're no different from anyone –

LEE: I know that.

MARINA: Well then –

LEE: I know that and sure. It's that – I *feel* different – and if there ain't no reason why such things happen and people become important and famous – there ain't no reason why it won't be me.

MARINA: You just sit there – and pretend . . . is that what you do?

LEE: You don't think things possible – because you don't think on them hard see – but I do – now I was *thinking* if I were to hijack a plane to Cuba – a good a real good plane and I'd stick the pilot with a pistol – he'd sure go there fast enough – then they'd pay attention to me . . . say that I'm a friend. I've got contacts now – my political allies write me from the North. But you wouldn't know about that . . .

MARINA: Why are you getting these letters from New York?

LEE: I am Chapter – for an organization.

MARINA: Oh – which?

LEE: Fair Play for Cuba.

MARINA: When are you going to work again?

LEE: When the unemployment money runs out. Meanwhile, I've got a job, I have an office, and I have printed headed notepaper which says Fair Play for Cuba – and you wouldn't understand.

MARINA: No – I wouldn't.

LEE: That's what I'm saying. And I'm saying something else – I want to take a trip – I have to go to Mexico City – because after all this work I've done for Cuba – when I go there – I'll get a visa – for Cuba – and I'll help them –

MARINA: Without me –

LEE: I'll come back before the cash runs down.

(*It is obvious* LEE *won't communicate with her. He is talking more to himself. Nothing she says cuts much ice in his mind.*)

MARINA: I can't stay here. I'll take June back to Dallas.

LEE: Yearh.

MARINA: Ruth Paine will have us.

(*She goes across to him. She takes the rifle from his still hands. She puts it on the table. All this is done very gently. The lack of contact fills the air between them.*)

You don't need this – if you go to Mexico . . .

(LEE *bows his head. He seems deeply upset.*)

LEE: No.

(MARINA *comes back to him. She touches his head. He won't move.*)

MARINA: Don't cry . . . Lee . . . things will be better things will be constant one day . . . I'm not nagging you.

(*Very gently she unstraps the pistol belt and holster from his waist. He is so hurt inside he cannot move. She puts it on the floor.*)

LEE: . . . You wouldn't understand . . .

MARINA: I try . . .

(*She unlaces and pulls off of him his heavy boots. They seem ridiculous and military and it is hot anyway.*)

LEE: The jobs – why do I lose them? . . . It would be much easier Marina in Russia – we wouldn't have to worry about tomorrow all the time – they look after you – you get work – all the time – and the State cares – the State wants you well and able – and here – it's run and jump – I been doing all of that – and – we get – a room and a television set – each time it's a start everything starts but it never finishes – that's what I'm saying.

(He is bitterly sad and ill about it. It's difficult to see if he cries or not, he hides his face. MARINA *kneels in front of him by the open window looking out on the New Orleans street.)*

When I told you in Minsk America was beautiful when I said it was wide open and exciting – I didn't tell you the truth. Nobody here takes care of you – you die here and it's only one less – you die in Russia and the State has lost an ally a friend . . .

MARINA: Come to bed . . .

LEE: Why?

MARINA: Come to bed and make love to me –

LEE: No Marina – you will never understand – I don't want to do that any more –

MARINA: Just sleep then –

LEE: Sleep is funny . . . I don't dream no more – I can't remember – but I know I'm sure – it's a black space now.

(The darkness again. Quite quickly MARINA *comes up front. The questions continue. She answers in a detached fashion. After all she has already been over this ground with the FBI. It is a repeat performance she doesn't enjoy.)*

COMMISSION: Did your husband stay with you at the Paines' after that first night when he returned from Mexico?

MARINA: Yes he stayed overnight there. And in the morning we took him to Dallas.

COMMISSION: And by 'we' who do you mean?

MARINA: Ruth Paine, I and her children.

COMMISSION: Do you know what he did in Dallas then?

MARINA: He intended to rent an apartment in the area of Oak Cliff, and to look for work.

COMMISSION: Do you know whether he did that?

MARINA: Yes I know that he always tried to get some work. He was not lazy.

COMMISSION: Did he rent the apartment?

MARINA: On the same day he rented a room, not an apartment, and he telephoned me and told me about it.

COMMISSION: Did you discuss the plans for this room before you took him to Dallas?

MARINA: No, I asked him where he would live and he said it

would be best if he rented a room, it would not be as expensive as an apartment.

COMMISSION: Did he say anything about whether you should be living with him, or he would be living there alone?

MARINA: No, I did not really want to be with Lee at that time, because I was expecting, and it would have been better to be with a woman who spoke Russian and English.

COMMISSION: Do you know where your husband looked for work in Dallas at that time?

MARINA: No. He tried to get any kind of work. He answered ads, newspaper ads.

COMMISSION: Did he have trouble finding work again?

MARINA: Yes.

COMMISSION: Did you discuss with him possible places of employment after his return from Mexico?

MARINA: No that was his business. I couldn't help him in that. But to some extent I did help him find a job, because I was visiting Mrs Paine's neighbours, there was a woman there who told me where he might find some work.

COMMISSION: And who was it that you got the information from?

MARINA: It was the neighbour whose brother was employed by the school book depository. He said it seemed to him there was a vacancy there.

COMMISSION: What was his name?

MARINA: I don't know.

COMMISSION: Mrs Oswald I do not ask these questions to pry into your personal affairs, but it gives us some insight into what he did and why he might have done the things he did . . . I hope you understand that.

MARINA: I understand.

COMMISSION: Could you tell us a little about when he did beat you because we have reports that at times neighbours saw signs of his having beat you, so that we might know the occasions and why he did such things.

MARINA: The neighbours simply saw that because I have a very sensitive skin, and even a very light blow would show marks. Sometimes it was my own fault. Sometimes it was really necessary to just leave him alone. But I wanted more attention. He was jealous. He had no reason to be. But he was jealous of even some of my old friends, old in the sense of age.

COMMISSION: When he became jealous did he discuss that with you?

MARINA: Yes of course.

COMMISSION: What did he say?

(*The stage lights up.* MARINA *is washing dishes. There is a knock on the door. Then a frantic knocking. She opens the door. It is* LEE. *If possible* MARINA *must appear pregnant at this time.*)

LEE: I want to talk . . .

MARINA: You can phone me.

LEE: I went to my post box this evening –

MARINA: Lee if you're going to start a quarrel – remember – Ruth is in this house and she is coming back and –

LEE: I want some truth!

MARINA: Yes?

LEE: Sit . . . sit . . .

(*He shoves her into a chair at a table. He takes the other chair and faces her across the table. He fetches an airmail letter and envelope out of the pocket in his jacket.*)

MARINA: I can't be made excited – I am about to have the baby –

LEE: You did not have my permission to use that box number of mine in the Dallas Post Office! Right – one! Two – this letter came back to the post box – today – two! And three – I read it . . .

MARINA: It – it was a joke –

LEE: I'll read it –

MARINA: It was – so help me – I'm telling you!

LEE: Dear Friend from out of the Russian past – when you asked me to marry you before I left Minsk – I made a big mistake – I remember how much you loved me – you said so –

MARINA: He was not my lover –

LEE: I am so happy to remember what it was like in the snow in the cold when we had nothing but fur boots and old woollen garments under our raincoats – here I am so miserable nothing ever seems to go right – people are not my friends – I move house too often –

MARINA: I was telling the truth –

LEE: I was a fool not to have married you – but now I cannot retrace my footsteps –

MARINA: Yes all right! I wrote it! . . . Damn you! Do you blame me – isn't it the truth – there is so little love between us?

LEE: Who was he – I mean is he?

MARINA: He loved me – once.

LEE: Behind my back – and let me tell you how I came by it you made one little mistake – you forgot the Texas postage duty has raised itself up one cent – last week! That's why they returned the letter to the box. My box!

MARINA: I have nothing to say. Except – he was a man and he loved me.

LEE: Why do you write to him?

MARINA: You tell me to leave you alone you tell me to go back to Russia that I'll be happier there – that there is nothing here in this huge vast country but small pay and your little jobs – now I begin to believe you!

LEE: But it's immoral to do that to me – write to him here – I'm your husband.

MARINA: Does it really still look like it to you Lee?

LEE: I try – I get work – I try.

MARINA: I have written letters before –

LEE: To him!

MARINA: To the Embassy in Washington – I take your advice I see it is hopeless – something drives you you fight everything – you hate at any given moment – there is no place for me in your life –

LEE: Tell me this – did you mean it sincere? All that letter?

(MARINA *pauses. She is afraid.*)

MARINA: . . . Yes.

(LEE *hits her across her head and hair. She sways.*)

LEE: Did you mean it for true?

MARINA: Yes . . .

(LEE *slaps her face very hard. The sound rings.*)

MARINA: . . . I deserve it . . . all right . . . I do.

LEE: There's more Marina . . .

(*He stands up.* MARINA *jumps clear and backs away.*)

MARINA: I have a baby now – you won't hit me again –

LEE: I've got to do something to you –

MARINA: Do anything – love me – do anything – but don't hit Marina – Alek!

(LEE *aims to hit her. She ducks away. She picks up a small portable radio. She hits him with it on the skull.* LEE *falls and catches his breath.*)

LEE: . . . Alek?

MARINA: I'm sorry . . .

LEE: Alek you called me . . .

MARINA: I always thought you were Alek when we first met – that was why.

LEE: That was years ago . . .

MARINA: Yes . . . I forget it all now . . .

LEE: You see . . . don't you . . . how jealous I am . . .

(*He seems like a child now. The energy has gone. He almost wants an adult's affection. He is self-righteous and suddenly rather soft and sullen.*)

MARINA: Of what Lee?

LEE: Our relationship.

MARINA: I wouldn't let you hit me – I think more of the baby than of you – what relationship is there now?

LEE: None – it seems all to have gone away . . . where did it go Marina – remember – and will you please tell me?

(*Then hold that. The stage darkens. Pause. Then* MARINA *comes forward. Spotlight.*)

COMMISSION: Did your husband continue to call you daily from Dallas after he got his job?

MARINA: Yes.

COMMISSION: Did he tell you what he was doing?

MARINA: Usually he would call me during the lunchbreak and the second time after he was finished work, and he told me that he was reading, that he was watching television, and sometimes I told him that he should not stay in his room too much, that he should go for a walk in the park.

COMMISSION: Have you ever heard that he used the fictitious name Hidell?

MARINA: Yes.

COMMISSION: Did you think he was using that assumed name in connection with this Fair Play for Cuba activity or something else?

MARINA: The name Hidell (Fidel) which you pronounce Hidell, was in connection with his activity with the non-existing organization.

COMMISSION: Now during the week of the assassination did your husband call you at all by telephone?

MARINA: He telephoned me on Monday, after I had called him on Sunday, and he was not there. Or rather, he was there but he wasn't called to the phone because he was known by another name. On Monday he called several times, but after I hung up on him and didn't want to talk to him he did not call again. He then arrived on Thursday.

COMMISSION: Did you learn he was using the assumed name of Lee as his last name?

MARINA: I know it now, but I did not ever know it before.

COMMISSION: Thursday was the 21st do you recall that?

MARINA: Yes.

COMMISSION: And the assassination was on the 22nd.

MARINA: This is very hard to forget.

COMMISSION: Did your husband give any reason for coming home on Thursday?

MARINA: He said that he was lonely because he hadn't come the preceding weekend, and he wanted to make his peace with me.

(*The stage lights up again.* MARINA *walks to a line. She stretches the line right across the stage and carefully places dozens of wet nappies on the line.* LEE *enters. He holds up a Coors beer*)

LEE: . . . Hi . . . Marina . . .

MARINA: Don't tread on the diapers . . .

LEE: I wasn't . . .

MARINA: You might.

LEE: . . . I said Hi . . . Marina . . .

MARINA: No 'Hi' Lee.

LEE: Means what?

MARINA: What I say.

LEE: Won't talk to me?

MARINA: No.

LEE: Well . . . I took the bus for an hour to come over here.

MARINA: Sure you did.

LEE: So that's an effort.

MARINA: I'm using Ruth's line in her kitchen to hang up diapers – that's one too.

LEE: Sure.

MARINA: . . . Sure.

LEE: But you won't talk –

MARINA: You know why I hung up – earlier –

LEE: No not really.

MARINA: Lee's not your real name –

LEE: No.

MARINA: Why tell lies about it?

LEE: I'm not hiding like – there's something immoral –

MARINA: Sometimes I wish there were! I'd understand you better.

LEE: I have to keep myself to myself –

MARINA: Surely. You do that.

LEE: I can't explain –

MARINA: Why didn't you come home over here – last week-end – ?

LEE: I thought you didn't want to see me.

MARINA: Do I now?

LEE: Marina . . . what if I were to get an apartment more in town – for us all –

MARINA: It's cheaper here. I don't spend your money.

LEE: What if – well the job's steady – I'll make peace with you Marina –

MARINA: Mind the laundry –

LEE: There'll be no more hitting you –

MARINA: There is no more – anyway.

LEE: I don't – I don't see any need why you should stay with Ruth – she ain't my friend –

MARINA: She's mine – she's good.

LEE: Look – haven't I played with the kids before? Course I have. Can I work regular – if they'll only let me hold on – sure I work. I want Rachel with me – and I want June – and you –

MARINA: You said it Lee – the hitting me, the rows, that gun thing and the Cuba – what happened with the visa? What has happened to me – do I go back – do I still apply to go home – and this name game – if you can't explain it who can? I'm tired Lee . . . be ordinary be normal be human – and something might happen – but everything falls apart and you can't see it!

(LEE *tries to move towards her. She ducks under the line. He pushes through it and pulls it down. The whole line. After she so carefully put it up. He treads clumsily on the wet nappies.*)

LEE: Oh Marina – I'm in a mess – I can't step over them –

(*They drape around him like a rash of wet white naval pennants.*)

MARINA: You see . . . how can I live? You're a mess – yes – but see how I live – if you want a hope – one brass hope in hell of getting me back – I want a machine –

LEE: A machine?

MARINA: I want one of those large washeteria machines – with a heater – with a spinner and a washing tub – and the electric wire and socket to make it work in – and then perhaps you won't tread all over my work! (*She furiously unravels the nappies from him. She strips them away from him. She gathers up the line*) That's it.

LEE: Then you'll have me?

MARINA: Maybe – the machine comes first.

LEE: That hurts – Marina.

MARINA: Good.

LEE: I try . . .

MARINA: Do it harder.

LEE: Is that all?

MARINA: There is no food to offer you.

LEE: I didn't mean that –

MARINA: I'm taking a bath – then I'm going to bed . . .

LEE: Oh I see.

MARINA: Goodnight Lee . . .

LEE: I'll be gone in the morning . . .

MARINA: Yes I know.

LEE: Gone early.

MARINA: I won't be awake.

LEE: . . . No.

> (*They stand and stare at each other. The light closes around them. The stage is dark now. Then after some seconds* MARINA *walks up front. The questions start.*)

COMMISSION: What did you do the rest of the morning after you got up on November 22nd?

MARINA: When I got up the television set was on, and I knew that Kennedy was coming. Ruth had gone to the doctor with her children and she left the television set on for me. And I watched television all morning, even without having dressed. June was running around in her pajamas watching television with me.

COMMISSION: Before the assassination did you ever see your husband examining the route of the parade as it was published in the paper?

MARINA: No.

COMMISSION: Did you ever see him looking at a map of Dallas like he did in connection with the Walker shooting?

MARINA: No.

COMMISSION: How did you learn of the shooting of President Kennedy?

MARINA: I was watching television, and Ruth by that time was already with me, and she said someone had shot at the President.

COMMISSION: What did you say?

MARINA: It was hard for me to say anything. We both turned pale. I went to my room and cried.

COMMISSION: Did you think immediately that your husband might have been involved?

MARINA: No.

COMMISSION: Did Mrs Paine say anything about the possibility of your husband being involved?

MARINA: No, but she only said that 'by the way, they fired from the building in which Lee is working' . . . My heart dropped. I then went to the garage to see whether the rifle was there, and I saw that the blanket was still there, and I said 'thank God'. I thought 'can there really be such a stupid man in the world that could do something like that?' But I was already rather upset at that time – I don't know why. Perhaps my intuition. I didn't know what I was doing.

COMMISSION: Did you look in the blanket to see if the rifle was there?

MARINA: I didn't unroll the blanket. It was in its usual position and it appeared to have something inside.

COMMISSION: When did you learn that the rifle was not in the blanket?

MARINA: When the police arrived and asked whether my husband had a rifle, and I said 'yes'.

COMMISSION: When the police came did Mrs Paine act as an interpreter for you?

MARINA: Yes.

COMMISSION: Did the police spend considerable time there?

MARINA: Yes.

COMMISSION: Did they want you to go with them?

MARINA: Yes.

COMMISSION: Did you leave the house with them right after they came?

MARINA: About an hour I think.

COMMISSION: And what were they doing during that hour?

MARINA: They searched the entire house.

COMMISSION: Did you see or speak to your husband on November 22nd following his arrest?

MARINA: On the 22nd I did not see him. On the 23rd I met with him.

COMMISSION: Did you request the right to see your husband on the 22nd after his arrest?

MARINA: Yes.

COMMISSION: And what answer were you given at that time?

MARINA: I was not permitted to.

COMMISSION: Where did you spend the evening on the night of the assassination?

MARINA: On the day of the assassination, on the 22nd, after returning from questioning by the police, I spent the night with Mrs Paine, together with Lee's mother.

(*She stands still. She is now very edgy and upset. The blow of* LEE *and his arrest shows in her. She breaks out from beneath this slow calm innocent and hesitant manner. Her emotions begin to bleed a little.*

Opposite her, on the other side of the stage, there is MARGUERITE. *She comes forward. The spot picks out her broad wrinkled troubled face. Much of the earlier confidence has left her too. The questions are directed at* MARGUERITE.)

MARGUERITE: . . . So then . . . the next thing we should start then . . . would be the Dallas . . . the assassination.

COMMISSION: Whatever you know.

MARGUERITE: Well, I was on a case in a rest home, and I had a three to eleven shift. I was dressed. Ready to go to work. I was watching – I'm a little ahead of my story, I watched the television in the morning before I was dressed. And Richard Nixon was in Dallas, and he made a television appearance approximately two hours before President Kennedy was to arrive in Dallas. And, as a layman, I remember saying – 'well, the audacity of him, to make this statement against President Kennedy just an hour or two before his arrival in Dallas'. And then I had my lunch, and I dressed, with my nurse's uniform on, to go to work, for the three to eleven shift. And I have to leave home at 2.30. So I had a little time to watch the Presidential procession. And while sitting on the sofa the news came that the President was shot. And there was a witness on television, a man and a little girl on television. However I could not continue to watch it. I had to report to work. So I went in the car, and approximately seven blocks away I turned the radio on in the car. I heard that Lee Harvey Oswald was picked up as a suspect. I immediately turned the car around and came back home, got on the telephone, called Acme Brick in Fort Worth, and asked where Robert was, because he had been travelling, and I must get in touch with Robert immediately, because his brother was picked up as a suspect in the assassination. So they had Robert call me. Robert didn't know that Lee was picked up.

COMMISSION: Was this the day of the assassination?

MARGUERITE: Yes sir. The day of the assassination they picked Lee up.

COMMISSION: And three to eleven – that is in the afternoon?

MARGUERITE: This was 2.30 because I was on my way to work, and I had to be at work at 3 o'clock.

COMMISSION: Three in the afternoon is when you had to be at work?

MARGUERITE: Yes sir. And it was 2.30 I heard the news and went back home. I had Acme Brick call Robert to give him the news, and Robert called me, and he had not heard his brother was picked up. Now Robert is in Denton. So I called the *Star Telegram* and asked that – if they could possibly have someone escort me to Dallas, because I realized I could not drive to Dallas. And they did. They sent two men to escort me to Dallas. The name of one is Bob Shieffer, the other name I will have for you gentlemen.

COMMISSION: Who are those? Are those reporters?

MARGUERITE: *Star Telegram* reporters, sent by the *Star Telegram* Editor to escort me to Dallas. Now upon arriving in Dallas, I did not ask – I did not want to talk to the police. I asked specifically to talk to FBI agents. My wish was granted. I was sent into a room. I have to backtrack my story. The policemen do not know I'm here – 'I want to talk to FBI agents!'

COMMISSION: This is approximately three thirty.

MARGUERITE: So I am escorted into an office, and two Brown FBI agents, they are brothers, I understand, and there was another man that I do not know the name.

COMMISSION: By that you mean that their names were Brown?

MARGUERITE: Their names were Brown. And I have the correct names, also. But we were in this room, and I told them who I was. And I said 'I want to talk with you gentlemen because I feel like my son is an agent of the government. And for the security of my country, I don't want this to get out' . . . But, first I said to them, 'I want to talk to FBI agents from Washington' . . . 'Mrs Oswald, we are from Washington, we work with Washington.' I said, 'I understand you work with Washington. But I want officials from Washington' – and I believed they would be in town because of protecting the President. I said – 'I do not want local FBI men. What I have to say I want to say to Washington men.' Of course, they wanted the news. They said 'Well, we work through Washington.' I said – 'I know you do. But I would like Washington men.' So I had no choice.

COMMISSION: Did you tell them why you thought he was an agent?

MARGUERITE: Yes sir, I am coming to this . . . So I said 'I have information that' – I told him who I was. I said – 'for the security of my country, I want this kept perfectly quiet until you investigate. I happen to know that the State Department furnished the money for my son to return back to the United States, and I don't know if that would be made public what that would involve, and so please will you investigate this and keep this quiet.' . . . Of course that was news to them . . . They left me sitting in the office . . . (*She seems to blurt all this out. As if she is hurried, as if something goads her along, words she feels she has to gobble out.*)

(*The stage becomes bright again. It is* RUTH PAINE's *home.* MARINA *is there sitting very sadly. The television set flickers dully.* MARGUERITE *hasn't seen* MARINA *for a year.* MARINA *speaks her pidgin English to* MARGUERITE. MARINA *has picked up English fairly well. She does seem to understand what people mean. Perhaps she doesn't understand when she doesn't want to know a point.*)

MARGUERITE: . . . Marina?

MARINA: Yes – Mamma.

MARGUERITE: I came as quick as I could.

MARINA: Oh yes.

MARGUERITE: Have you been crying?

MARINA: All day . . .

MARGUERITE: I have too.

MARINA: They all came here.

MARGUERITE: Who 'they' honey?

MARINA: The officers.

MARGUERITE: The police?

MARINA: They come . . . bang bang – all noise.

MARGUERITE: Now it's quiet.

MARINA: Yes Mamma. .

MARGUERITE: Do you need any help?

MARINA: No.

MARGUERITE: Some food – cook a meal?

MARINA: No thank you.

MARGUERITE: He didn't do it – my Lee never done.

MARINA: Mamma – he had gun.

MARGUERITE: Everybody has a gun in Dallas –

MARINA: And he had mind – gone!

MARGUERITE: Don't you let them talk you in on anything –
(MARINA *gets up. She crosses to a shelf. On the shelf is a thick book. She takes a photograph out from the book. She hands it to* MARGUERITE.)

MARINA: Mamma – I show you.

MARGUERITE: Did you take that?

MARINA: Me.

MARGUERITE: Holding this rifle and all – and the pistol –

MARINA: Read it Mamma.

MARGUERITE: It says – to my daughter June.

MARINA: Yes.

MARGUERITE: Have you shown this anyone?

MARINA: No. You take it Mamma –

MARGUERITE: No.

MARINA: You have it –

MARGUERITE: No Marina . . . put it back in the book. Please.
(MARINA *does so. Silently.*)

MARINA: Mamma – you stay here with me? Yes.

MARGUERITE: Yes – thank you.

MARINA: Ruth won't mind.

MARGUERITE: Marina – have you seen him?

MARINA: No.

MARGUERITE: Has he got a lawyer – he's a member of Civil Liberties.

MARINA: I don't know.

MARGUERITE: Do you want to see him honey?
(MARINA *doesn't answer. As if she hasn't heard the question. She looks back at her mother-in-law. She doesn't say a word. The stage darkens.* MARINA *stands forefront. The questions begin again.*)

COMMISSION: But from what you have learned since that time

you arrived at this conclusion, did you, that your husband had killed the President?

MARINA: Yes, unfortunately, yes.

COMMISSION: And you related those facts that you learned to what you already knew about your life with him and what you knew he had done and appeared to be doing in order to come to that conclusion?

MARINA: Yes.

COMMISSION: When you saw your husband on November 23rd, at the police station, did you ask him if he had killed the President?

(MARINA *steps back into the stage. We can see* LEE *standing behind a glass wall. He looks lost and rather unkempt. Very haggard.* MARGUERITE *stands near to* MARINA. MARINA *approaches* LEE *first. She picks up the communicating telephone.*)

MARINA: . . . Hallo Lee . . .

LEE: Hallo.

MARINA: I tried to see you yesterday . . .

LEE: Yes I know. I guessed.

MARINA: Hallo Lee – June is well . . .

LEE: Don't worry don't worry . . . don't cry.

MARINA: I love you . . .

LEE: Good. Fine.

MARINA: There is love?

LEE: From me? Sure . . . yes.

MARINA: I don't believe . . . that you did that – and everything –

LEE: I know what you're trying to say –

MARINA: Everything – everything will turn out – well.

LEE: Yes.

MARINA: And I love –

LEE: I do. I do.

MARINA: I hear you . . .

LEE: Don't worry about a thing – as you say – it will all turn out – hear me?

(MARINA *puts the telephone down, and walks away from the glass wall. She stands apart and away.* MARGUERITE *walks up to the glass wall.*)

MARGUERITE: . . . Honey you are so bruised up. Your face.

What are they doing?

LEE: Mother don't worry now. I got that in a scuffle.

MARGUERITE: Is there anything I can do to help you?

LEE: No, Mother. Everything is fine. I know my rights. And I will have an attorney. I have already requested to get in touch with Attorney Abt, – I think is the name. Don't worry about a thing.

MARGUERITE: I won't ask you a thing Lee . . . I am with you that's all.

LEE: I didn't do it Mother – I didn't do it. Now go home – tell Marina to buy June new shoes – go home – go now.
(*They all three leave the stage. After a pause* MARINA *walks back in on her own. The lights go down. A light centres on* MARINA.)

COMMISSION: Do you know whether he was ever acting as an undercover agent for the FBI?

MARINA: No.

COMMISSION: Do you believe that he was at any time?

MARINA: No.

COMMISSION: Do you know whether or not he was acting as an agent for the CIA at any time?

MARINA: No.

COMMISSION: Do you believe that he was?

MARINA: No.

COMMISSION: Did you know Jack Ruby, the man that killed your husband?

MARINA: No.

COMMISSION: Before the murder of your husband by Jack Ruby, had you ever known him?

MARINA: No, never.

COMMISSION: Do you know whether your husband knew Jack Ruby before the killing?

MARINA: He was not acquainted with him. Lee did not frequent nightclubs, as the papers said.

COMMISSION: How do you know that?

MARINA: He was always with me. He doesn't like other women. He didn't drink. Why should he then go?

COMMISSION: Do you know any reason why Jack Ruby killed your husband?

MARINA: About that, Jack Ruby should be questioned.

COMMISSION: I have to ask you Mrs Oswald.

MARINA: He didn't tell me.

(*From the other side of the stage* MARGUERITE *comes forward. The light fades on* MARINA. MARGUERITE *is talking. She is trying to make something clear, something which to her is very important. She seems excited as if she has discovered the truth.*)

MARGUERITE: . . . now just a minute gentlemen, because this I know is very important to me and to you, too. We had been in the jail. This was an evening. Well this then would be approximately five thirty or six in the evening.

COMMISSION: What day?

MARGUERITE: On Saturday November 23.

COMMISSION: That was at the Executive Inn?

MARGUERITE: At the Executive Inn. Now Mr Hart Odum, the FBI agent, knocked on the door at the Executive Inn. I had my robe and slippers on, and I pushed the curtain aside when he knocked. He said 'This is Mr Odum.' I opened the door just a little, because I had the robe off and I didn't want anybody to come in. He said 'Mrs Oswald we would like to see Marina.' I said 'Mr Odum I am not calling my daughter. As a matter of fact she is taking a bath.' She wasn't. He said 'Mrs Oswald I would like to ask you a question.' The door is ajar. I wear bifocals which enlarges things. And in his hand – in the cup of his hand, like this is a picture. He said 'Have you ever seen this man before?'

(*The lights are on the whole stage area.* MARGUERITE *walks to the door. She is wearing a nightrobe. She speaks to the far side of the door. Opposite her* MARINA *is unrolling a pair of stockings from her legs. She has no apparent interest in the conversation at the door.*)

MARGUERITE: . . . Mr Odum . . . I stated yesterday you are not going to see Marina.

(*There is a muffled sound of a male voice behind the door.*)

You see – we are awful tired. Now you see.

(*Again the sound of a man's inquiring voice.*)

As a matter of fact she is taking a bath.

(*She seems to take a clear black and white photograph from behind the door. She looks at it carefully. The muffled male voice*

212

continues. She hands the photograph back behind the door)
. . . No sir . . . believe me. I have never seen this picture in my life.

(She closes the door. She leans against it. She looks across at MARINA. MARINA *totally unconcerned inspects the ladders in her stockings. The light fades again.*

MARGUERITE *walks up front. She talks again to the* COMMISSION.*)*

COMMISSION: Could we get what picture this is? Is that the picture held in the hand?

MARGUERITE: Yes sir – the picture that is held in the hand, that the FBI agent Mr Hart Odum showed me.

COMMISSION: I understand you didn't recognize who the picture was at all.

MARGUERITE: No. I told Mr Hart Odum I had never seen the man before – 'believe me sir' – and he left. So the picture was shown – was tried – had tried to be shown to my daughter-in-law but they were not successful. Now I am under the impression since I know it was Mr Jack Ruby's picture I saw – at the time I didn't.

COMMISSION: How do you know that?

MARGUERITE: I have seen his picture in the paper. Now I know it is Mr Jack Ruby.

COMMISSION: What was the date now?

MARGUERITE: This Saturday November 23rd. This is approximately 6.30 in the evening that the FBI agent came. And the telephone call was later. Now I have no way of knowing whether Lee had permission to use the phone, remember Lee is in jail.

COMMISSION: About what time do you think that telephone call was?

MARGUERITE: I would say it was about 7.30, 8 o'clock in the night.

COMMISSION: That was still on Saturday night?

MARGUERITE: Yes sir. Still on Saturday night at the Executive Inn. And that was after the picture was shown to me – she received this telephone call, and became very silent. And the next day my son was shot.

COMMISSION: Do I understand correctly that Marina did not see the picture at any time?

MARGUERITE: That is correct sir. But they tried awfully hard for Marina to see the picture.

COMMISSION: And when they could not show it to her –

MARGUERITE: – they showed it to me – yes sir.

COMMISSION: Have you ever seen that picture since?

MARGUERITE: – Lee was shot on a Sunday – neither Marina nor I knew how he was shot. They kept it from us. You have to visualize this. We were at the Six Flags Motel with approximately eighteen to twenty FBI agents, secret service men running in and out a woman with a Russian girl and two sick babies, and the girl and I do not know what is going on.

COMMISSION: Now, about what time on that Sunday did you learn of your son's death?

MARGUERITE: Well now, here is your time element. I said Robert and Mr Gregory and the Secret Service were there approximately from 11.30. And I knew nothing about the shooting. And then we had to go to Irving and everything. Then they told us Lee was shot. So now we are bringing up to the time – it all fits in – which was 1 o'clock or 1.30. And they were all watching the sequence on television . . .

(*The stage lightens.* MARGUERITE *goes across to a TV set which is flickering. It stays on the exit in the Dallas Police carport and basement where Lee Oswald was to be taken out to a waiting car.*
MARGUERITE *sits down on what looks like a very plain piece of hotel-type motel kind of seating arrangement. The TV set flickers. An American voice says out loud 'And here he is. Here is Lee Harvey Oswald. Lee Harvey Oswald the number one suspect in the assassination of the President . . . here he is . . . he is . . .' The voice describes the scene which is suddenly terminated in the violent gunshot from Ruby's pistol above the noise and press of the crowd in the basement.*
MARGUERITE *springs round. She doesn't quite stand up. She looks desperate, as if light has hit her in between the eyes. The sound of the TV set whirs in the background.* MARGUERITE *is in pain. She is full of indignation and confusion. As she understands it some terrible hoax has been performed.*

Behind her on the TV set we can hear the name Jack Ruby being called out frequently. The commentator pans desperately with his camera to get a shot of Ruby.

MARGUERITE *rears round, as if she is addressing the crowded room she is in, in the Six Flags Motel TV room.)*

MARGUERITE: . . . That's him! . . . That is the man! Do you hear me? I'm saying – he was the man in that photograph – ask Marina – ask her in Russian – she was there – I was told I was shown that man's face yesterday – last night – and I understand now – too clearly – you'd have to kill me too – I want to make a statement I want to make a statement! I'm Marguerite Oswald – I'm Lee Harvey's mother – I must be heard! The boy is a hero – not a murderer!

(She rises to her feet. She is alone on the stage. She looks so awfully alone and tired, and beaten down with her own imaginings real or unreal. Her heavy little body sweats. She shakes. She wants to cry. She wants to show. She must have her say. All those around her seem so alien. All they want to do is protect little MARINA. *Only she speaks alone. A pause. After the silence, the darkness descends again.* MARGUERITE *like a beast in pain somewhere reels in the blackness.*

Out from the dark steps MARINA. *This time she wears a simple neat cotton dress. She looks a little worried.)*

COMMISSION: Now Mrs Oswald it has been necessary to ask you back to Washington on account of the recent news story which I believe the *Houston Post* ran claiming your husband also tried to shoot Mr Richard Nixon. On the final day of your testimony, we asked you – do you remember any information or documents under your control or in your possession which would relate to or shed any light on the matters we have been examining which you have not presented here? And you replied 'I have nothing else. Everything has been taken from me.' Now Mrs Oswald it has been made necessary to recall you in the light of the new evidence.

MARINA: There were an awful lot of questions at that time, and I was very tired, and felt that I had told everything and I don't remember, I can't understand why I didn't mention this. It would have been better for me to mention it the first time than to make you all do more work on it.

(*She steps back on the stage.*

The lights come up. There is a bed. LEE *is swiftly putting on a suit. Beside the bed is a bathroom door.*)

MARINA: . . . That's your suit Lee.

LEE: Yearh . . . sure it is.

MARINA: Is there a wedding?

LEE: There might be a funeral.

(*He picks up his pistol from the bed. He carefully places it in his waistbelt.*)

MARINA: I don't understand you –

LEE: Nixon's coming into town this morning –

MARINA: Oh. So what?

LEE: So I'm going to see –

MARINA: Not with that gun –

LEE: I'm going to see Nixon – and will you leave me alone.

MARINA: Why the gun?

LEE: He's a bad man. That's why.

(*He goes into the bathroom. He shuts the door. There is the sound of tap water running.*)

MARINA: (*Shouts*) Lee you're not going – not like that – remember what I said after General Walker was shot at –

LEE: (*Off*) No.

MARINA: I said I'd go right on down to the police and inform them of you. I can't live with you like this –

(*As* LEE *opens the door to come out,* MARINA *grabs at the handle. She pushes the door inwards.* LEE *tries to push the door outwards in its correct direction. They struggle.*)

LEE: Get away from that door –

MARINA: Not until you say you won't kill!

LEE: Marina – I'm warning you now!

(*He manages to push the door out on to the stage.* MARINA *has to back away. As he comes out she lunges for the gun in his waistband. He fights with her.*)

MARINA: Lee . . . don't . . .

LEE: I want to be left! I . . .

(*He suddenly sags. He relaxes.* MARINA *takes the pistol. She looks at him.*)

I won't fight with you –

MARINA: No. I'm a woman.

LEE: Give me my gun back.

(MARINA *throws it on the bed. He walks to it. She stands in front of him.*)

MARINA: You won't go out –

LEE: I won't go out –

(*She lets him pick up the pistol.*)

MARINA: You'll stay home.

LEE: You are always getting in my way.

MARINA: You'll do what I ask.

LEE: I will not take the gun. But I am going out sometime – I'm going to go out and find if there is an appropriate opportunity and if there is I will use the pistol.

(*The stage darkens.* MARINA *comes back up front.*)

COMMISSION: Had it come to your attention Mrs Oswald that Mr Nixon was going to be in Dallas prior to that time?

MARINA: No, I did not.

COMMISSION: Had you seen anything in the newspapers or heard anything over the radio or television?

MARINA: No we didn't have TV I didn't see that in the newspaper. I did not think up this incident with Nixon myself.

COMMISSION: What do you mean by that Mrs Oswald?

MARINA: It might have been that he was just trying to test me. He was the kind of person who could try and wound somebody in that way. Possibly he didn't want to go out at all, but was just doing this all as a sort of joke, not really as a joke, but rather to simply wound me to make me feel bad.

COMMISSION: Do you recall the bathroom, how the door closes? Does it close into the bathroom on Neely Street or from the outside in?

MARINA: I don't remember now, I don't remember. I only remember that it was something to do with the bathroom.

COMMISSION: Did you lock him into the bathroom?

MARINA: I can't remember precisely.

COMMISSION: Do you recall how the locks were on the bathroom door there?

MARINA: I can't recall. We had several apartments and I might be confusing one apartment with the other.

COMMISSION: Is it your testimony that you made it impossible for him to get out if he wanted to?

MARINA: I don't remember.

COMMISSION: Did he try to get out of the bathroom?

MARINA: I remember that I held him.

COMMISSION: He is quite a big man and you are a small woman?

MARINA: He is not a big man, he is not strong.

COMMISSION: Did you have some fear that he would use the weapons against someone else?

MARINA: Of course, I was afraid.

COMMISSION: You thought that he might use his weapons against someone?

MARINA: After the incident with Nixon I stopped believing him.

COMMISSION: You what?

MARINA: I stopped believing him.

COMMISSION: Why?

MARINA: Because he wasn't obeying me any longer, because he promised and then he broke his promise.

(*All through this particular piece of recall evidence* MARINA *seems ill at ease. It is obvious she doesn't know now in her own mind whether she invented this story or whether her mind at the earlier session with the Commission just couldn't focus on this Nixon episode.*

MARINA *stays where she is. The stage is now very bare. The lights come up. There stands* MARINA *on one side, on the other side stands* MARGUERITE. *They both stare out at the audience.* MARGUERITE *as of ever blurts out her own statement. She just stands there and says it as if she is waving a flag.*)

MARGUERITE: . . . You see we have two sides here. It is a very serious charge, because no one saw him shoot at the President. And the Commission has come to the conclusion that Lee Harvey Oswald has shot President Kennedy, and he alone. Lee Harvey Oswald or Mr J. Lee Rankin, or anyone in this room, could not have been in that many places in twenty-nine minutes time. It is utterly impossible. I have 1,500 letters sir – not just letters of sympathy, people that are investigating this. But he step by step has been taken, from what the reports said – that he was on the sixth floor, and then they saw him in the cafeteria drinking a Coca-Cola, and the President came. Then he had to leave the building. He had so many blocks to walk before he caught a bus. He had to board the bus, he had to pay his fare, he had to get out of the bus, then he walked a few blocks, then he caught a taxi-cab, then he paid the taxi man, then he walked a few blocks went to his home and got a coat. Then he walked a few more blocks and shot the policeman. Then he walked a few more blocks and he was in the theatre. In twenty-nine minutes time it cannot be done. (*She just stands there and says it. She is near calm. Not wholly so.*)

(MARINA *is very calm, cool and at ease. She doesn't seem very troubled by the breadth of the questions. Behind them both the stage is quite empty. Any small pieces of set have gone away. It is bleak and very very empty. Just the two women standing there.*)

COMMISSION: Mrs Oswald this question has already been asked you but I would like to ask it again. I gather that you have reached the conclusion in your own mind that your husband killed President Kennedy.

MARINA: Regretfully yes.

COMMISSION: During the weeks and months prior to the assassination – and I think this question has also been asked – did you ever at any time hear your late husband express any hostility toward President Kennedy?

MARINA: No.

COMMISSION: What motive would you ascribe to your husband in killing President Kennedy?

MARINA: As I saw the documents that were being read to me – I came to the conclusion that he wanted in any – by any means, good or bad, to get into history. But now that I have heard a part of the translation of some of the documents, I think that there was some political foundation to it, a foundation of which I am not aware.

COMMISSION: By that, do you mean that your husband acted in concert with someone else?

MARINA: No, only alone.

COMMISSION: You are convinced that his action alone, that he was influenced by no one else?

MARINA: Yes I am convinced.[1]

COMMISSION: Do you consider your husband a communist?

MARINA: He told me when we were in New Orleans that he was a communist, but I didn't believe him, because I said, 'what kind of a communist are you if you don't like the communists in Russia?'

COMMISSION: Did he like the communists in the United States?

MARINA: He considered them to be on a higher level and more conscious than the communists in Russia.

COMMISSION: Did you consider your husband a normal man in the usual sense of the word?

MARINA: He was always a normal man, but where it concerned his ideas, and he did not introduce me to his ideas, I did not consider him normal.

COMMISSION: Maybe I used the wrong terminology. Did you consider him mentally sound?

MARINA: Yes he was smart and capable. Only he did not use his capabilities in the proper direction – he was not deprived of reason – he was not a man deprived of reason.

(MARGUERITE *from the far side simply talks at the audience. She doesn't hear* MARINA. *She hears no one. Her words are very emotional. She finds meanings in almost the most trivial phrase.*)

MARGUERITE: . . . So I am convinced my son, and my son alone, if he is involved, I am a human being, and I say my son could have shot the President, and he could have been involved. I am not the type mother to think that he is perfect and he could not do it. But I say he did not do it alone – if he did it. Because it is utterly impossible. And I do not believe my son did it. I think my son was framed because, gentlemen, – would his rifle be in the sixth floor window of the depository – unless you want to say my son was completely out of his mind. And yet there has been no statement to that effect. Wade has publicly said on television when it happened that he is sane, he is well reasoned, he knows what he did. And Lee never did break, with his black eyes. He kept saying that

---

1 The interchangeable sequence, pp. 149–51, can be placed here.

he was innocent. And yet in twelve hours time he was proven guilty . . . That doesn't make sense to me an ordinary layman. So I have to consider who is involved. Now I am telling you that this girl was not happy with her situation. She had turned against me twice . . . You, yourself, yesterday said that she testified that I told her to tear up the picture of Lee with those guns. God give me the Grace – I did no such thing. My testimony is true. So now she has lied there, I have found out . . . And every evidence of any importance has come from this house. I have to face that.

(*She is still now. She has finished. The mother stands rather limply. There are tears there. The voice is smashed and tired. The mother holds her face in her hands dramatically. Perhaps she means it to seem like that. She covers her eyes. She is empty and exhausted and bone still.*

MARINA *waits for the question again. She is calm and tired. Her clothes are tidy and pretty. Her face is a Jackie Kennedy mask. The makeup and the hairstyle.*)

COMMISSION: Now let me ask you one other question; assuming that this is correct, would you feel that there would be any less guilt in killing Governor Connally than in killing the President?

MARINA: I am not trying to vindicate or justify or excuse Lee as my husband. Even if he killed one of his neighbours, still it wouldn't make much difference – it wouldn't make any difference – a killing is a killing. I am sorry . . .

END

FOR THE BEST IN PAPERBACKS, LOOK FOR THE

In every corner of the world, on every subject under the sun, Penguin represents quality and variety – the very best in publishing today.

For complete information about books available from Penguin – including Puffins, Penguin Classics and Arkana – and how to order them, write to us at the appropriate address below. Please note that for copyright reasons the selection of books varies from country to country.

In the United Kingdom: Please write to *Dept E.P., Penguin Books Ltd, Harmondsworth, Middlesex, UB7 0DA*.

If you have any difficulty in obtaining a title, please send your order with the correct money, plus ten per cent for postage and packaging, to *PO Box No 11, West Drayton, Middlesex*

In the United States: Please write to *Dept BA, Penguin, 299 Murray Hill Parkway, East Rutherford, New Jersey 07073*

In Canada: Please write to *Penguin Books Canada Ltd, 2801 John Street, Markham, Ontario L3R 1B4*

In Australia: Please write to the *Marketing Department, Penguin Books Australia Ltd, P.O. Box 257, Ringwood, Victoria 3134*

In New Zealand: Please write to the *Marketing Department, Penguin Books (NZ) Ltd, Private Bag, Takapuna, Auckland 9*

In India: Please write to *Penguin Overseas Ltd, 706 Eros Apartments, 56 Nehru Place, New Delhi, 110019*

In the Netherlands: Please write to *Penguin Books Nederland B.V., Postbus 195, NL–1380AD Weesp*

In West Germany: Please write to *Penguin Books Ltd, Friedrichstrasse 10–12, D–6000 Frankfurt Main 1, Federal Republic of Germany*

In Spain: Please write to *Longman Penguin España, Calle San Nicolas 15, E–28013 Madrid*

In France: Please write to *Penguin Books Ltd, 39 Rue de Montmorency, F-75003 Paris*

In Japan: Please write to *Longman Penguin Japan Co Ltd, Yamaguchi Building, 2–12–9 Kanda Jimbocho, Chiyoda-Ku, Tokyo 101*

FOR THE BEST IN PAPERBACKS, LOOK FOR THE

PLAYS IN PENGUIN

Edward Albee   **Who's Afraid of Virginia Woolf?**

Alan Ayckbourn   **The Norman Conquests**

Bertolt Brecht   **Parables for the Theatre (The Good Woman of Setzuan/The Caucasian Chalk Circle)**

Anton Chekhov   **Plays (The Cherry Orchard/Three Sisters/Ivanov/The Seagull/Uncle Vanya)**

Henrik Ibsen   **Hedda Gabler/The Pillars of the Community/The Wild Duck**

Eugène Ionesco   **Absurd Drama (Rhinoceros/The Chair/The Lesson)**

Ben Jonson   **Three Comedies (Volpone/The Alchemist/Bartholomew Fair)**

D. H. Lawrence   **Three Plays (The Collier's Friday Night/ The Daughter-in-Law/The Widowing of Mrs Holroyd)**

Arthur Miller   **Death of a Salesman**

John Mortimer   **A Voyage Round My Father/What Shall We Tell Caroline?/ The Dock Brief**

J. B. Priestley   **Time and the Conways/I Have Been Here Before/An Inspector Calls/The Linden Tree**

Peter Shaffer   **Lettice and Lovage/Yonadab**

Bernard Shaw   **Plays Pleasant (Arms and the Man/Candida/The Man of Destiny/You Never Can Tell)**

Sophocles   **Three Theban Plays (Oedipus the King/Antigone/Oedipus at Colonus)**

Arnold Wesker   **Plays, Volume 1: The Wesker Trilogy (Chicken Soup with Barley/Roots/I'm Talking about Jerusalem)**

Oscar Wilde   **Plays (Lady Windermere's Fan/A Woman of No Importance/ An Ideal Husband/The Importance of Being Earnest/Salome)**

Thornton Wilder   **Our Town/The Skin of Our Teeth/The Matchmaker**

Tennessee Williams   **Sweet Bird of Youth/A Streetcar Named Desire/The Glass Menagerie**